Bible Stories that Scared the Hell out of Me

Jay W. Foreman

Copyright © 2024 by Jay W. Foreman, Stephens City, VA

All rights reserved. No part of this publication may be reproduced, distributed, or transmitted in any form or by any means, including photocopying, recording, or other electronic or mechanical methods, without the prior written permission of the publisher, except in the case of brief quotations embodied in critical reviews and certain other noncommercial uses permitted by copyright law.

ISBN (Paperback): 979-8-9913611-3-2
ISBN (Hardcover): 979-8-9913611-4-9
ISBN (eBook): 979-8-9913611-2-5

First Impressions

"I don't know what your experiences with God have been, or what you understand of the many teachings and stories in the Bible, but it's probably safe to say that we all have much to learn. If the Bible is the primary source for learning Who God is and what He is like, it would serve us well to read it, study it, and discover what it teaches us about Him. But there are some stories that are just weirder than others, and at first glance seem inconsistent with what we think we know about God and the spiritual realm. I love how Jay tackles these odd and off-putting stories, giving thoughtful insight so the reader can gain an understanding and make an application. Sharing his own struggles and his sense of humor, Jay encourages us to give these stories a second look and maybe gain a fresh appreciation for Who God is and what He might really be up to."

Eric Reploeg
Pastor at Virginia Hills Church

"If you have ever read the Bible and been left scratching your head, this book is a great resource for you! Jay does an excellent job walking through difficult passages of Scripture that he finds scary or confusing. He takes you on a journey of how he made sense of the stories in a fun and relatable way. Every chapter ends with meaningful and practical applications for your everyday life."

Ryan Miller
Pastor at Canvas Community Church

"This book will Biblically inform and jovially entertain ALL who read it! From Boomers to Zoomers, this book will keep you interested and entertained, as Jay shares Bible stories, scriptures, and life experiences that answer some of those head-scratching questions we've all had along our spiritual journeys! Whether you're new to The Faith, or a "seasoned" Christ follower, if you're looking for an enriching read that isn't stuffy, but is more like you're eating wings and nachos and talking Bible stories and scripture in your favorite comfortable setting, this book is for you!"

Jared Nail,
Christ follower

"Jay and I grew up together and went to the same church. It has been such a breath of fresh air to learn more about the depths of Jay's faith as I read through the pages of his book. We all have questions. Just like Jay, I'm amazed at how all the words of the Bible came together and how they amazingly tell a story of hope and salvation. Jay does a splendid job of displaying certain stories that cause some fear, maybe even confusion, for many of us. Jay equally does a fantastic job of giving some really well-thought-out answers. I found myself laughing at many comments that folks who share the same upbringing in the 80s will find humorous too. I found myself, scratching my head in curiosity about the unique stories of God's Word. Mostly, I found myself deeply moved at God's love for me, for all of us. And when you read it to the end, you will also be moved to tears of joy at the thought of being welcomed home by Jesus."

Dennis Dale
Pastor of Adult Discipleship at Faith Community Church
Fort Atkinson, Wisconsin

"Countless people have walked this earth searching for meaning and purpose. For many, they end up dying, never realizing that their life was to Glorify their creator with the time that God gave them. They spend all their energy chasing after a vain quest to become something God never intended. He only wanted them to genuinely know and experience His love for them and that He never makes mistakes when God creates anything. He is the potter, and we are the clay. When we wrestle with God, we only fight with God's perfect will for our lives.

As a theologian, pastor, church planter, son, father, and husband for almost 30 years, I can genuinely attest to Jay's wisdom in this line from chapter 4 of Let's Get Ready to Rumble: A Story of Jacob.

"God rarely gives us yes or no answers, but He always hears us and, in His time, helps illuminate what He has called us to do and where He has called us to go."

God longs for us to embrace His love and purpose for our lives. This can be best summed up in Psalms 23:6 NLT: "Surely your goodness and unfailing love will pursue me all the days of my life, and I will live in the house of the Lord forever."

I truly believe that this book will foster a deep love for God's Word and an appreciation for the crazy, creative way God shows up throughout history and continues to reveal himself to us in the everyday moments of our lives. I highly recommend Bible Stories That Scared the Hell Out of Me by Jay W. Foreman."

Pastor Lee Reams

Dedicated to Bailey,
my one family member who has never critiqued my writing!

All Scripture quoted in this book is taken from the
New Century Version translation unless otherwise noted.

Table of Contents

Foreword xi
For Your Consideration xiii
Preface xv
A Father's Love 1
A Donkey's Dangerous Diatribe 8
Bad News Bears 15
Let's Get Ready to Rumble 21
The Demon Who Knew His Role 30
A Serpent's Ceaseless Seduction 39
More Malchus Please 45
Snake Handling 101 52
May I Follow? 59
What's in a Name? 65
Biblical Oxymorons? 72
Too Much Studying May Be Hazardous To Your Health 80

I Never Knew You..87
Easter Saturday 96
Hair Today, Gone Tomorrow 101
The Original Walking Dead 110
Why Doesn't God's Script Match Mine?...................116
Angels Among Us...122
God > Behemoth + Leviathan....................................129
Saul's Scary Situation 136
A Curious Case of Context 146
You'll Never Go in The Water Again........................152
The Revelation of Revelation 162
Surprise Party...170
Final Thoughts 175

Foreword

I met author Jay Foreman in 2010 while working on one of his first books at another publishing company. Being in Indiana and seeing that Jay lived in Virginia, I was surprised when his email address had the phrase "IndyColtsGuy" in it. I guess you can say this is how our friendship began. Over the years we've experienced the highs…but mostly lows, of being fans of the Colts, but it's the bond of sports that brought us together in the first place. I suppose it was only fitting that when I got the call from Jay asking if I would write the Foreword for this book, I was on my way to coach a baseball game, in Indianapolis, of all places. As honored as I was to be asked to do this, I can assure you that the pages you read after this one will be far more enjoyable!

In this book, Jay has taken Bible stories that most of us already know by heart and found a creative way to help us contemplate what we *thought* we already knew. As you read along, you will have flashbacks to when you were a kid and hopefully find a way to get a little more out of these stories than you previously did as a child.

When I was in college, I was a part-time youth leader at my church. I really didn't know what I was doing, but I kept thinking I had to find a way to get them to youth group, even if I wasn't much of a biblical scholar. Keeping them laughing was always my "go-to" approach. Humor has always been something Jay and I share together, although our wives rarely understand just how funny WE are, not to mention how lucky THEY are! If you are reading a book of Jay's for the first time, you will see his sense of humor shine through, and it will feel as if you know him personally.

I hope this book allows you to go back to a simpler time. A time when you were hearing these stories for the first time as a kid, or perhaps even as an adult. I also ask that you take these stories to heart and use a combination of scripture and Jay's words to help reflect and take a deeper dive into the purpose of these stories being included in the Word of God. I assure you that you will come out a stronger believer and that you will be looking forward to Jay's next book!

I've already mentioned how Jay and I have a bond through sports and humor, but in all honesty, it's our commitment to Christ that is our most important bond. You will see it shine through these next pages as you read along.

In closing, thank you Jay for letting me be a part of this journey. It is truly an honor and one that I will always remember. Go Colts!

Brian W. Martindale
VP of Author Relations
Genesis Publishing House

For Your Consideration

I consulted several pastor friends of mine as I wrote and edited this book. Through several of them, I was reminded that the Bible was written both *to* us and *for* us. Both classifications are imperative to our growth as followers of Christ. In this book, I focus on the aspects of how the Bible is written *to* us. Meaning that I believe God speaks directly to us through His word. We can read the same passage at different stages of our lives, and God may deliver different takeaways for us. God continues to meet us where we are and gives us the guidance we need. This happens through prayer, fellowship, and in this case, the Bible. The stories in Scripture become very personal and relatable when we allow them to.

But I also want to share that the Bible is written *for* us as well. Meaning that God tells a wonderful fully-connected story through His word. Some refer to it as the Grand Narrative. The four main chapters of the Grand Narrative include Creation, Fall, Redemption, and Restoration. Simply put, God created the world. Sin was introduced. God gave His Son so that we may be saved. God will restore creation at some point in the future. This story is written *for* us. It's our guide to what has happened, what is happening now, and what the future holds. Every story in the Bible fits into the Grand Narrative. They're there to complete the story. I wanted to share this, because as much as I focus on the Bible stories that scared me as a kid and what they mean to me now, it's even more important that we understand God's full story to the best of our abilities. That's why I have included discussion questions at the end of each chapter, the last question focusing on how the previous story fits into the Grand Narrative.

While reading this book, my prayer is that you study these stories, hopefully enjoying my commentary on what they mean to me, but even more so, contemplating what God is communicating to you personally while obtaining a better understanding of where they all fit into the Grand Narrative.

Preface

The year was 1982. I was ten years old. I had just graduated third grade. As a reward for achieving this milestone, I, along with my fellow classmates, was presented a pristine Good News Bible during church service. I was so excited. It had a cool-looking picture of a shepherd rescuing a sheep on the cover. And inside, it was inscribed to me personally. I knew I was going to cherish this book for the rest of my life. After church was over, there was a covered-dish luncheon to continue the celebration of the young men and women who had earned their new Bibles. As usual, my buddies and I wolfed down our fried chicken, deviled eggs, and Jell-O salad, so we could head outside and play football. Everyone left their Bibles with their parents, except me. I was proud of my latest possession. After all, I earned it! I didn't want it to leave my sight just yet. I took it with me and laid it on the hood of a nearby parked car.

We played football, tackled each other, stained our Sunday clothes, and had a great time. I remember catching the game-winning touchdown pass, but my celebration was cut short. As soon as I got ready to spike the football, I saw the car on which I had laid my Bible, tear out of the parking lot. Time stood still as I watched my immaculate book launch off the vehicle and twist and turn in the air before crashing down hard on the concrete pavement. There, it tumbled a few more times before coming to a stop, the cover completely scuffed and more than a few pages torn. My brand-new Bible…completely ruined. The over-reactor in me immediately began questioning why bad things happen to good people. I picked up my raggedy Bible and stared down at it. What do I do with it now? Was I even allowed to throw a Bible in the trash? Then, out of nowhere, my pastor showed up. He looked at the Bible. Then at me. And said something I've never forgotten.

"Way to break in your Bible!"

Was he kidding? I wasn't in the mood for jokes. And also, that wasn't even funny. Then he followed up with another line that changed my life.

"A Bible that's falling apart usually belongs to someone who isn't."

I've since learned that this was a Charles Spurgeon quote. But it doesn't matter if the line was borrowed or not. It had a major impact on me at a young age. It helped me to be less superficial and worry more about what's inside the Bible than its exterior. And it also led me to spend more time in the Bible. After all, I certainly didn't want my life falling apart. So, I started reading more. And not just the stories that we covered in Sunday School. And it turned out there was A LOT we didn't cover in Sunday School. Now I understand why. There is some scary stuff in scripture. Some of these tales were confusing. And some of these accounts kept me up at night.

A lot of the stories you're about to read, whether for the first time or for the hundredth time, can come off sounding rather bizarre. But that comes from reading them at a surface level. Much like Jesus' parables, the stories of the Bible are complex, with multiple layers and lessons. This is one of the many reasons the Bible is so re-readable. It's easy to cover the same story again and again, yet discover something new or different each time.

God doesn't want us to simply read the stories of the Bible. He wants us to inhale them. He wants His word to be our oxygen. He wants it to consume us and breathe new life into us. Once we take time to read past the words on the page and process the *why* of the story, our eyes are opened. And once we really start understanding and appreciating the stories being told, we start to notice that many of the characters in the Bible are a lot like us. Yes, the Bible was written thousands of years ago, but the principles in it are just as relevant today as they were then.

I hope you enjoy the Bible stories in the pages ahead, along with my commentary on the lessons God revealed to me. You may read these same stories and leave with different takeaways. That's the beauty and the power of the Bible. Hebrews 4:12 reminds us,

God's word is alive and working and is sharper than a double-edged sword.

The Bible is *alive and working*. God always seems to be using it to share with each of us the message we need to hear at the exact time we need to hear it. So, dive into the pages ahead, relive some of the scarier stories of the Bible, and listen for what God is trying to teach you from them. Enjoy!

CHAPTER 1

A Father's Love
A Story of Abraham and Isaac

For the first chapter of this book, I decided to start with some low-hanging fruit. This is by far the one Bible story that scared me more than any of the others combined. This one literally kept me up a night or two as a kid. It's the story of Abraham and Isaac. Before we dive in, allow me to give you a quick backstory on Abraham. He had a very special relationship with God where God actually spoke directly to him.

Abraham is one of God's chosen few. One of His favorites. One of His *golden boys* as I like to refer to them. He is one of the original characters of the Bible through which God chose to accomplish wonderful and miraculous feats. I refer to Abraham as a *golden boy,* but the truth is…I don't think God plays favorites. Even though I opened a fortune cookie one time that read, *"God Loves You Especially,"* it didn't take long for me to realize that this fortune was meant for me…and another thirty thousand Chinese food fans who would be receiving this mass-produced fortune. The truth is that God doesn't have a *good ol' boy* system from which he chooses His teammates. The only criteria for being chosen by God to do great things are to show up and to be available to Him. There...it only took me two paragraphs and I'm already off topic. Back to Abraham and Isaac. Genesis 22:1 – 18 paints the picture.

> *¹After these things God tested Abraham's faith. God said to him, "Abraham!" And he answered, "Here I am." ² Then God said, "Take your only son, Isaac, the son you love, and go to the land of Moriah. Kill him there and offer him as a whole burnt offering on one of the mountains I will tell you about." ³Abraham got up early in the morning and saddled his donkey. He took Isaac and two servants with him. After he cut the wood for the sacrifice, they went to the place God had told them to go. ⁴ On the third day Abraham looked up and saw the place in the distance. ⁵ He said to his servants, "Stay here with the donkey. My son and I will go over there and worship, and then we will come back to you." ⁶ Abraham took the wood for the sacrifice and gave it to his son to carry, but he himself took the knife and the fire. So he and his son went on together. ⁷ Isaac said to his father Abraham, "Father!" Abraham answered, "Yes, my son." Isaac said, "We have the fire and the wood, but where is the lamb we will burn as a sacrifice?" ⁸ Abraham answered, "God will give us the lamb for the sacrifice, my son." So Abraham and his son went on together ⁹ and came to the place God had told him about. Abraham built an altar there. He laid the wood on it and then tied up his*

son Isaac and laid him on the wood on the altar. [10] Then Abraham took his knife and was about to kill his son. [11] But the angel of the Lord called to him from heaven and said, "Abraham! Abraham!" Abraham answered, "Yes." [12] The angel said, "Don't kill your son or hurt him in any way. Now I can see that you trust God and that you have not kept your son, your only son, from me." [13] Then Abraham looked up and saw a male sheep caught in a bush by its horns. So Abraham went and took the sheep and killed it. He offered it as a whole burnt offering to God, and his son was saved. [14] So Abraham named that place The Lord Provides. Even today people say, "On the mountain of the Lord it will be provided." [15] The angel of the Lord called to Abraham from heaven a second time [16] and said, "The Lord says, 'Because you did not keep back your son, your only son, from me, I make you this promise by my own name: [17] I will surely bless you and give you many descendants. They will be as many as the stars in the sky and the sand on the seashore, and they will capture the cities of their enemies. [18] Through your descendants all the nations on the earth will be blessed, because you obeyed me.'"

And there you have it…what I used to refer to as the scariest story in the Bible. As a kid, can you blame me? I was brought up in a Christian household where I was taught that God still speaks to us (maybe not directly like He did with Abraham, but He speaks to us, nonetheless). So, you know what was running through my adolescent mind each night. *What if God sends the same command to my dad that he sent to Abraham? And what if the Angel of the Lord is taking a coffee break and doesn't intervene in time?* It's easy for me to laugh about it today, but as a kid, these questions consumed more of my thoughts than I should have allowed.

Now don't get me wrong. I didn't obsess over this. It wasn't like I was double-checking the kitchen knife rack before I went to bed at night to make sure no blades were missing. And I wasn't constructing a Coke can-pyramid in front of my bedroom door, so that if I had an unexpected guest approach in the middle of the night I would be alerted to the fact before any sacrifices could take place. But this story *did* weigh heavily on me.

Once I got a little older, I quit worrying about becoming a sacrifice. But then another thought entered my mind. What if God calls me to sacrifice *my* son one day? Would I be able to do that? I had no idea what it would be like to be a father at this stage of my life, but I doubted I'd have the intestinal fortitude to complete a task like this. Then I became a little angry that I might be asked to carry out such a heinous crime to begin with. I wondered how this whole scenario reflected God's character. What kind of God would ask for a father to carry out this despicable act against his own son?

It wasn't until I was a little older (not wiser, just older)…and a little more mature in my faith that I decided to revisit this story. I read it again and again and prayed about it. And it was as if the lenses through which I had been reading this story as a child were given a new prescription. I started seeing this scene play out in a completely different light. Yes, God ordered Abraham to kill his beloved son, Isaac. Yes, Abraham agreed to do it.

Yes, Abraham raised that knife above his son's prone body and looked him in the eyes. Yes, I'd imagine both were in tears at this point. And the most definitive Yes of all: Yes, God stopped it from happening.

I had been so caught up for years in the first part of this frightening series of events that I neglected the ending. God asked Abraham to perform the unthinkable. But He also makes sure that the unthinkable doesn't occur. God knows the powerful bond there is between father and child. He created it. And he knew that it would be devastating for Abraham to sacrifice someone he loved so dearly. And while God would not allow Abraham to experience that kind of pain and grief, it's exactly what God Himself would go on to do later on the cross at Calvary.

To that end, I think this story serves as a foreshadowing in the Bible (which is a lot of what the Old Testament is all about). God watched the same sacrifice that He had stopped Abraham from making hundreds of years before, occur before His very eyes. Only this time, it was *His* son who was being sacrificed. This act could have been stopped, too. God could have easily pulled His son off the cross. Jesus had the authority to pull the plug on this action as well. But out of pure unadulterated love, the ultimate sacrifice was made for you and me. What God would not allow Abraham to do because of the sorrow it would bring was the exact same thing He did to save us all.

It's funny that for years, I took the self-righteous approach as I thought of the story of Abraham and Isaac and was appalled by the outrageousness of God possibly allowing a human sacrifice. Yet, too often, when I think of the story of Jesus' crucifixion and resurrection, I look at it as a great story where He beat death and saved a wretched sinner like me in the process. I'm so excited about what I gained that I lose sight of what God gave up.

As I continue to grow in my faith (and believe me…it's a long journey), I don't perceive God's call to Abraham to be as outlandish as I used to. I can't fathom being asked to sacrifice my own son, but I can now put this directive into perspective. How many times do we receive a calling from God and respond with, *Are you kidding me?* Like God telling Abraham to sacrifice his own son, how many times has God spoken to your heart to perform an act that either makes no sense or takes you a few hundred miles outside of your comfort zone? I don't know about you, but it happens to me more often than I'd like to admit. The next time you feel like God is completely off the mark in what He's asking you to do or where He's asking you to go, remember the story of Abraham and Isaac. On the surface, the call from God made no rational sense, but Abraham responded. He showed up, ready to act. And what happened? God had his best interests at heart. And he was blessed.

If there is something God is calling you to do that you're struggling with, take a page out of Abraham's playbook. Show up and be willing to do the job. God will take it from there.

Discussion Questions

1. Is there anything in your life right now that you feel God may be calling you to do? Are you resistant? If so, why? What's holding you back?

2. Think back. Do you remember a time when you trusted God when it didn't make sense to do so? What happened?

3. How do you think the story of Abraham and Isaac fits into the Grand Narrative?

CHAPTER 2

A Donkey's Dangerous Diatribe
A Story of Balaam

A lot of folks don't realize that Shrek's loveable sidekick is not the first talking donkey recorded in history. The original talking donkey can be found in the book of Numbers at the beginning of the Bible. For some reason, this story was never discussed in any of my Sunday School classes when I was a kid. I may have paid more attention on Sunday mornings if these were the kinds of stories we were discussing. It wasn't until I was an adult that I read this passage.

I'll set up the scene you're about to read. The Israelites were becoming a powerful force to be reckoned with and the Moabites were next in line for an altercation. They decided to try and hedge their bets by appealing to a sorcerer named Balaam, who supposedly had influence with God. Balak, the King of Moab, sent his older leaders to visit Balaam (with a blank check for him to fill in the amount) and asked him to curse the Israelites so that they wouldn't cause any problems for them. At first, Balaam rejects their plea, but eventually decides to go with them to meet with Balak. Check out Numbers 22:21 – 34.

> ^{21}*Balaam got up the next morning and put a saddle on his donkey. Then he went with the Moabite leaders.* ^{22} *But God became angry because Balaam went, so the angel of the Lord stood in the road to stop Balaam. Balaam was riding his donkey, and he had two servants with him.* ^{23} *When the donkey saw the angel of the Lord standing in the road with a sword in his hand, the donkey left the road and went into the field. Balaam hit the donkey to force her back on the road.* ^{24} *Later, the angel of the Lord stood on a narrow path between two vineyards, with walls on both sides.* ^{25} *Again the donkey saw the angel of the Lord, and she walked close to one wall, crushing Balaam's foot against it. So he hit her again.* ^{26} *The angel of the Lord went ahead again and stood at a narrow place, too narrow to turn left or right.* ^{27}*When the donkey saw the angel of the Lord, she lay down under Balaam. This made him so angry that he hit her with his stick.* ^{28} *Then the Lord made the donkey talk, and she said to Balaam, "What have I done to make you hit me three times?"* ^{29} *Balaam answered the donkey, "You have made me look foolish! I wish I had a sword in my hand! I would kill you right now!"* ^{30} *But the donkey said to Balaam, "I am your very own donkey, which you have ridden for years. Have I ever done this to you before?" "No," Balaam said.* ^{31} *Then the Lord let Balaam see the angel of the Lord, who was standing in the road with his sword drawn. Then*

Balaam bowed facedown on the ground. ³² The angel of the Lord asked Balaam, "Why have you hit your donkey three times? I have stood here to stop you, because what you are doing is wrong. ³³ The donkey saw me and turned away from me three times. If she had not turned away, I would have killed you by now, but I would have let her live." ³⁴ Then Balaam said to the angel of the Lord, "I have sinned; I did not know you were standing in the road to stop me. If I am wrong, I will go back."

After reading this for the first time, I shook my head, trying to envision the story I had just read. Now, I believe God is the God who parted the Red Sea to help the Israelites escape. I believe God is the God who decided to give Meshach, Shadrach, and Abednego flame-retardant skin once they were thrown into the furnace. I also believe that God is the God who was in that infamous den and made sure Daniel was a lion's friend instead of his dinner. I can easily picture all of these miracles occurring, but for some reason, I had to seriously concentrate on seeing this one unfold in my mind.

Why? Was this miracle harder to pull off for God? Of course not! Jeremiah 32:27 tells us, "I am the Lord, the God of every person on the earth. Nothing is impossible for Me." After much reflection, it occurred to me why I was having trouble with this *stranger than fiction* scene of God using a talking donkey. It's because it wasn't on a grand scale like the other phenomena to which I was comparing it. It just didn't send a bold message like these other miracles.

When an ocean literally split, and thousands of Israelites crossed to safety while thousands of pursuers drowned on the back end, a statement was made to the remaining Egyptians. When Shadrach, Meshach, and Abednego proved to be fireproof and Daniel proved to be lion-repellant, a statement was made to the on-looking Babylonian governors, assistant governors, soldiers, royal advisors, and others in the crowd. These were great miracles that affected many people. God's supreme power was evident and unquestionable. It's safe to say that these particular miracles, among many others, changed the course of history.

So, what's up with a talking donkey? Sure, a donkey talking is nothing short of a miracle, but it's not like the aforementioned ones. There's not a lot of drama. In fact, in my opinion, there's more comedy than anything else. There's not a grand stage for many to witness the proceedings. Who knows if this miracle changed the course of history like the others did? After all, this was simply a conversation between a man and his mule.

After dwelling on this passage for a while, it became a little clearer to me. God's miracles don't always take place on grand stages. He's shown that they *can*, but when it comes down to it, I think most of His miracles take place in smaller venues, with fewer people...even audiences of one. He continues to work in our individual lives each and every day. That's how much He loves us. The miracles are there if we just look for them.

But let's get back to Balaam for a moment. Why did God provide his donkey with the gift of gab? In my opinion, it's a demonstration that God will use whatever means are necessary to grab our attention and get through to us. It may be a gut feeling, advice from a friend, a good book, a billboard, a movie, skywriting, or even a talking animal. He knows us and He knows the best way to communicate in the most effective manner possible. Now, most of us would probably not need God to send a talking donkey to grab our attention, but reread the verse where the donkey talked for the first time.

> *[28] Then the Lord made the donkey talk, and she said to Balaam, "What have I done to make you hit me three times?" [29] Balaam answered the donkey, "You have made me look foolish! I wish I had a sword in my hand! I would kill you right now!"*

Did you catch that? The donkey *talks*. For the first time in history, a donkey talks and asks Balaam a question. What does Balaam do? He *answers* her! He doesn't stand there, awe-struck. He doesn't turn to his buddy and ask, *"You heard that too, right? It's not just me, is it?"* No. Balaam is so self-centered at that moment that he is not even fazed by the donkey's voice. In fact, he's so unaffected by the back-and-forth, in his anger, he threatens to kill the donkey!

It's not until the donkey points out the angel with the sword standing in their path that Balaam comes to his senses and recognizes the seriousness of the situation. I don't know why, but I always picture this angel in the road as the bad guy who swings his sword around for show right before Indiana Jones shoots him in *Raiders of the Lost Ark*.

Even this scene is another microcosm of the way a lot of us live our lives. God puts people (and even animals) in our lives sometimes to help us head down a specific road that He has planned for us. These folks are in our lives to help keep us on the right path. I don't know how many times I have failed to listen to these friends and family members in my own life, only to find myself off the path, or worse…to the wrong destination. These are the times we see what God was trying to keep us away from. They may not always be as blatant as an angel carrying a sword, but they can be just as negatively consequential.

Think about the people in your life that God has given you. And I'm not talking specifically about Christians. I'm talking about everyone that's in your life that's important to you. God uses everyone for His purposes. Are you listening to the ones that you know love you and want what's best for you? Remember verse 30 from the story where the donkey reminds Balaam that she has his best interest at heart.

But the donkey said to Balaam, "I am your very own donkey, which you have ridden for years. Have I ever done this to you before?

So, what do I take away from this story when I read it these days? Three bullet points:

1. Even if you were the only person on the planet, God would still perform miracles just for you.
2. God is the God of creativity. Don't ever underestimate the lengths He will go to in order to communicate with you.
3. We all have *donkeys* in our lives that God has given us to help teach, encourage, and even save us from time to time. Look *for* them and look *to* them when you need guidance.

Discussion Questions

1. Was there a time when you felt like God used unconventional means to get your attention? What happened? Did it work? How did you respond?

2. Do you believe God loves you enough to speak to you in ways that He knows will have an impact? Are you actively listening for God's guidance?

3. How do you think the story of Balaam's donkey fits into the Grand Narrative?

CHAPTER 3

Bad News Bears
A Story of Elisha

The next Bible story that we'll cover is one that I consider the most bizarre of them all. And by bizarre, I mean at first glance the story seems out of place and unnecessary. Coincidentally, it's another scene from the Bible that my Sunday School teachers conveniently omitted when I was a child. And I don't blame them. This one's a little hard to wrap my head around as an adult. Who knows what a child's takeaway from this story would be? It features the prophet, Elisha. He is a good man, and just like Jake and Elwood Blues, he's on a mission from God. 2 Kings 2:23 – 24 shares this.

> *²³ From there Elisha went up to Bethel. On the way some boys came out of the city and made fun of him. They said to him, "Go up too, you baldhead! Go up too, you baldhead!" ²⁴ Elisha turned around, looked at them, and put a curse on them in the name of the Lord. Then two*

mother bears came out of the woods and tore forty-two of the boys to pieces.

If it's been a while since you've visited this passage, go ahead and take a moment to process it. After my first twenty or so initial readings of it, I couldn't help but form more questions than answers. Not only did the story seem to not fit, but it also made no sense. I'm supposed to accept that a grown man got his feelings hurt by a few kids who were just goofing around? Then I'm supposed to accept that he put a curse on them? A curse, mind you, by our God, who is also synonymous with love. And finally, I'm supposed to accept that our loving God unleashes two grizzlies on these poor innocent children and watches as they tear them limb from limb? If you're like me, that's too much to digest and it flies in the face of everything else the Bible tells us about God. This was my first reaction. And it stuck with me for a while. But after a little research into this story, I started to view it in a different light.

Upon further examination, this story isn't bizarre at all. It's symbolic of what happens when we agree to let God work in us and through us. Elisha received his marching orders from the Lord and was on his way to Bethel to minister to the people living there. It was ironic because while Bethel meant *house of God* or *place of God,* the city had become very evil. As he got to the outskirts of town, a welcoming committee who appeared to be anything but, meets him. In some translations, including the New Century Version used earlier, these folks are referred to as *boys* or *children*. In other translations, the term *lads* is used. The Hebrew translation of *lad* is *naar* which can be used to describe servants or soldiers. So, we don't know for sure if these were in fact children or a group of soldiers waiting for Elisha.

And what do they do when they see him? They call him names. This may seem a bit childish, and it is, but notice *how* they verbally attacked him. They made it personal. They said to him, *"Go up too, you baldhead! Go up too, you baldhead!"* Now I don't know if Elisha was actually bald, had just gotten a bad haircut, or was just unfortunate enough to live in an era before hair plugs, but the group made fun of his appearance. To reiterate, in the immortal words of the good guy in every 80s action movie ever...*they made it personal!*

And that's what can happen when you try to do what's right. Your personal nature can be attacked. And it's not fun. They weren't attacking his mission. They weren't attacking his God. They were attacking *him*! And even though they're just words, I can tell you from experience that being attacked personally hurts. Whether what's being said is true or not. I have written several books, and with each published book comes new reviews. Some are good. Some are bad. That's the nature of the business and I'm fine with that. But I'll tell you this...it's much easier to stomach a review that questions how good my latest book is than a review that questions how good I am as a writer. Why? Because one is about my work, and one is about *me*.

But Elisha decides to take the high road. He doesn't engage them in a war of words. There are no *"I know you are, but what am I?"* chants going back and forth. He doesn't challenge them to a fight (one at a time obviously), either. What does he do instead? He turns the situation over to God by putting a curse on them. You've heard the term, *Let go. Let God?* It's exactly what Elisha did, which by the way, is a lot easier said than done. Since we're on the topic of the curse, let's examine it a little more closely. When I used to think of a *curse in the name of God,* I'd imagine some incantation like, *"Get 'em God! Do your worst!"* But that's not how God works. That's more of a scene from *Aladdin* with his magic genie. A curse in God's name refers more to what Peter talks about in 1 Peter 2:23.

> *People insulted Christ, but he did not insult them in return. Christ suffered, but he did not threaten. He let God, the One who judges rightly, take care of him.*

The curse was more of a, *"Hey God...you're seeing this situation, right? Do what needs to be done for me to carry out Your will."* And that's exactly what happened. But why the drama? Why did God call on two bears to tear out of the woods and attack these folks? My guess is this. This was a drastic time and it called for drastic measures. Remember, there were forty-two guys blocking Elisha's path. This was basically a mob. They weren't peacefully assembled, and they weren't going to let Elisha pass without some sort of altercation. And hey...if God can use a talking donkey, why not a couple of hungry bears?

Another part of me thinks that this feeding frenzy straight out of a horror movie played another role. I think that if there were any other opponents of Elisha waiting around just in case the first forty-two somehow failed, they received the message loud and clear regarding the consequences of interfering with God's message being delivered to this town. I can see Elisha yelling out, *"Who's next?"* with a bear on each side of him, standing on its hind legs, toothpicks hanging out of their mouths. Okay, I know this is ridiculous and I also realize that I watch way too many cartoons for my age. But I *do* think a clear message was sent with this encounter.

It's a message that is just as relevant in our lives today as it was in Elisha's back then. When God speaks to us and calls us to do something, we have a chance to be part of a wonderful experience. Sometimes he calls us by combining our passions and our talents. Other times he calls us by taking us out of our comfort zones. There appears to be no rhyme or reason for how or when he calls us. But I believe there is a very miraculous method to His madness and one day it will be revealed to us. But until then, He simply asks us to trust Him. And I believe He's given us this story as a reminder that when we work for Him, we shouldn't be intimidated by the challenges in life. We shouldn't be discouraged by the setbacks, either.

Just like with the obstacle Elisha was facing, when we give our struggles to the Lord, He doesn't just whisk them away quietly. He tears them to pieces to remind us that He is in control. And when we trust in Him to work through us, it's not a matter of *if* His plan will succeed, it's a matter of *when* His plan will succeed. With God on our side, we're a majority. It's just hard to believe that sometimes today. So, the next time you're feeling dejected or defeated in trying to live the way God wants you to live, remember to give your problems to Him and watch Him unleash the bears in your life!

Discussion Questions

1. Reflect. Do you recall a time when God removed an obstacle from your life? Do you recall a time when God gave you the strength to overcome an obstacle?

2. Do you trust God to obey Him and try to carry out His will for your life? If you're hesitant, why do you think that is?

3. How do you think the story of Elisha and the bears fits into the Grand Narrative?

CHAPTER 4

Let's Get Ready to Rumble
A Story of Jacob

Of all the stories in the Bible that confused me once upon a time, the story of Jacob and his infamous wrestling match is at the top. Depending on what translation of the Bible you read or which pastor or theologian you confer with, Jacob was either wrestling with an angel of God or God Himself. I remember shaking my head in dismay that God or one of his representatives would come down to Earth and actually *wrestle* with a mere mortal. I could buy into God or an angel showing himself to Jacob in some miraculous, grandiose form and bestowing some words of wisdom on him. But actually having a knock-down, drag-out, good old-fashioned *rasslin'* match? Something just didn't add up. But wait…my confusion didn't end with the wrestling match itself. I had several post-match questions as well. I'll get to those in a moment. First, let's revisit the passage at hand from Genesis 32:22-32.

²² During the night Jacob rose and crossed the Jabbok River at the crossing, taking with him his two wives, his two slave girls, and his eleven sons. ²³ He sent his family and everything he had across the river. ²⁴ So Jacob was alone, and a man came and wrestled with him until the sun came up. ²⁵ When the man saw he could not defeat Jacob, he struck Jacob's hip and put it out of joint. ²⁶ Then he said to Jacob, "Let me go. The sun is coming up." But Jacob said, "I will let you go if you will bless me." ²⁷ The man said to him, "What is your name?" And he answered, "Jacob." ²⁸ Then the man said, "Your name will no longer be Jacob. Your name will now be Israel, [a] because you have wrestled with God and with people, and you have won." ²⁹ Then Jacob asked him, "Please tell me your name." But the man said, "Why do you ask my name?" Then he blessed Jacob there. ³⁰ So Jacob named that place Peniel, [b] saying, "I have seen God face to face, but my life was saved." ³¹ Then the sun rose as he was leaving that place, and Jacob was limping because of his leg. ³² So even today the people of Israel do not eat the muscle that is on the hip joint of animals, because Jacob was touched there.

Before I get into my other questions regarding the actual wrestling match, allow me to give you my take on whether Jacob's opponent was actually God or an angel. As I stated before, there are arguments and valid cases for both cases, but in my humble opinion (and please remember, that is all this is, my opinion), Jacob was wrestling that fateful night with none other than…drum roll, please…God. My reasons? First of all, verse 28 tells us that Jacob's name was changed to Israel, which when translated, literally means: *he wrestles with God*. Secondly, after it was all said and done, Jacob named the area where the bout had taken place: Peniel. The translation of Peniel is *the face of God*. But the real reason I think it was God who was wrestling is something else altogether. And I'll get to that at the end of this chapter. For now, let's look at some of the bizarre questions that can be plucked from this fight.

Are we really supposed to believe that God realized He couldn't beat Jacob?

If so, doesn't God come across as a poor sport by putting Jacob's hip out of joint?

Why wouldn't God tell Jacob who He was when Jacob asked?

Three valid questions. Now allow me to provide three answers. (You can decide the validity of them for yourself.) Are we really supposed to believe that God couldn't beat Jacob in a wrestling match? Of course not! This is God we're talking about. I feel God was trying to teach Jacob a lesson about himself. God had plans to use Jacob for great things. Yet, Jacob had yet to prove his worth. In fact, Jacob had a habit of running away from troubles instead of dealing with them like a man. He cheated his brother, Esau, out of a blessing from their father and then ran away instead of facing Esau. Later, after some shady business dealings with his Uncle Laban, Jacob ran away again rather than face the consequences. Jacob had established a pattern of not only making messes in his life but also not owning up to them. He would hear God but would not always follow His instructions.

It's not a coincidence that Jacob had just recently prayed to God, asking for strength and deliverance as his encounter with his brother, Esau, loomed on the horizon. This wrestling match was God's answer to prayer. He showed Jacob the futility of not listening to Him, or in other words, *wrestling with God*. Whether it is physical or metaphorical, wrestling with God gets us nowhere and it wastes time. Reliance on God is what gives us true strength, not wrestling with Him. They apparently wrestled all night before that lesson sank in for Jacob.

Jacob went from trying to fight a battle there was no way he could win to doing the only thing he could…hold on to God. Remember, God could have pinned Jacob or made him tap out or do whatever it was they did in those times to end the match. But He didn't. He stuck with Jacob until the lesson was learned and the message was received. That's the essence of God. He's not a quitter. And He doesn't want us to be quitters, either. He stayed engaged with Jacob, just like He stays engaged with us until we receive His message.

That's what happened here. Jacob stopped wrestling and simply clung to God. There was nothing else he could do. And he found out that by clinging to God, there was nothing else he needed to do. As a well below-average high school wrestler, I can relate to this desperation measure very well. I'm not kidding about being a poor wrestler in my youth. I still remember our cheerleaders taking their break during my matches. They knew they'd have nothing to cheer for when I was on the mat. Anyway, once I realized I had no chance of winning my match (typically about forty-five seconds into the first period), I would simply wrap up my opponent's leg and hang on for dear life.

This lame technique accomplished two goals for me. It didn't allow my opponent to escape from me. And it prevented my circumstances from getting any worse. And that's exactly what Jacob was trying to accomplish by holding on to God. He didn't want to be apart from God and he didn't want his situation to worsen, which on the surface looked like it was about to. Often in our lives, especially at the low points, all we can do is cling to God. And by showing us this match, He's allowing us to see that a lot of the time, clinging to Him is all it takes.

Now that we have some insight into the reason for the marathon match, it's time for the second question. What's with the injury to the hip? The lesson was taught and received. End of story. What purpose did this serve? One popular theory is that this was simply a reminder that whenever we truly encounter God, we don't remain the same. Or perhaps it was a reminder for Jacob to always remember to rely completely on God and not on his own doing. Paul would experience something similar to this later in the Bible when he had a problematic situation in his life so bad that he begged God on three separate occasions to remove it from him. Check out the Lord's response from 2 Corinthians 12:9-10.

> *⁹ But he said to me, "My grace is enough for you. When you are weak, my power is made perfect in you." So I am very happy to brag about my weaknesses. Then Christ's power can live in me. ¹⁰ For this reason I am happy when I have weaknesses, insults, hard times, sufferings, and*

all kinds of troubles for Christ. Because when I am weak, then I am truly strong.

Let those last words sink in for a moment. *When we are weak, we are truly strong.* When we realize we can't do it on our own and then commit who we are to God, that's when our true strength is realized. This reminds me of one of my favorite quotes from G.K. Chesterton. *"Anything done in our own strength will fail miserably or succeed even more miserably."*

And let's not underestimate the significance of the time of day that the wrestling match ended. The sun was coming up. It was the dawning of a new day. This was symbolic of a new beginning. Jacob was a changed man. He had a new heart. A new relationship with the Lord. A newfound reliance. A new name. And a new injury to prove it. The darkness was gone, and it was time for Jacob to step into the light with a fresh start. Once again, God proving that He's the King of second chances.

So, for the last question, and maybe the most mind-boggling one of them all, why didn't God just tell Jacob His name when asked? I think the answer is profound. I believe it was God's way of saying, *"You know who I am. I don't need to confirm anything."* I love this scene because it reminds me of the way God works in our lives today. Just like Jacob, He doesn't answer me directly, either. But when I come to Him in genuine prayer, He makes sure I hear an answer somehow. A lot of the time, as in the case of Jacob, we already know the answer to the question we're asking. We're either scared to hear the answer or are hoping we're wrong. But deep down, our gut usually steers us in the right direction. And by *gut*, I mean the Holy Spirit working within us.

One of my favorite stories of God answering me indirectly happened many years ago. Book sales had slowed to a snail's pace. Nobody was looking to book a motivational speaker whose repertoire was limited. And my author visits to schools were becoming fewer and farther between. As a result, so were paydays. I took my situation to God in prayer. *"God,"* I began, *"I honestly feel like the whole 'author-speaker-teacher' road you've sent me down is where you're calling me to be, but we both know that I need to provide for my family, too. If it's time for me to suck it up and go back to one of my previous jobs in corporate America, just help me to see that and to follow your guidance."* I prayed this right before bedtime and then dreamt that night of being back in my cubical at Freddie Mac, where I had worked a decade before.

As soon as I woke up, I realized I was sweating. My stomach hurt, I was cold and clammy, and I was scared. God had spoken to me. Obviously, He wanted me to start my commute again and apply for my old job of pushing papers and…well, to be honest, I never really was quite sure what it was I did there. Instead of being humbled and thankful that God took the time to answer my prayers, I immediately dropped to my knees and started praying again. *"But God…it's not all about the money, right? I'm getting by and can learn to stretch a dollar a little more. And did you forget about how many hours I'd be in the car each day commuting? That's time away from family. You're surely not condoning that, are You? And if I stop what I'm doing now, I definitely won't be using any of the spiritual gifts you've blessed me with, so that's no good..."* And the groveling and the excuses and the pandering went on and on and on. Until on came the proverbial light bulb. It was suddenly abundantly clear to me.

I didn't want to do anything else. I wanted to continue writing. I wanted to speak more often and at bigger venues. I wanted to teach more often. God used this dream to show me where my real feelings lay. I was just at a bump in the road, not a dead end. The journey may have been rough and lonely and disappointing, but it was one that He helped me realize I wanted to keep heading down. God rarely gives us yes or no answers, but He always hears us and, in His time, helps illuminate what He has called us to do and where He has called us to go. Just like with Jacob, often He'll ask, "Why do you want to know?" And more often than not, when we search the *why* of our question, we'll find that God has already blessed us with His answer. He wouldn't tell Jacob who He was because He knew that Jacob already knew.

So, there you have it...my post-match commentary from a wrestling bout that could have main-evented any WrestleMania in the last forty years!

Discussion Questions

1. Have you ever *wrestled* with God? What was it about? What was the outcome?

2. Are there any areas of your life where you may need to *tap out* to God and turn things over to Him?

3. How do you think the story of Jacob's wrestling match fits into the Grand Narrative?

CHAPTER 5

The Demon Who Knew His Role
A Story of Legion

The next story I'd like to visit is one that used to make the hairs on the back of my neck stand up when I read it. Looking back, I now know that it scared me because it gave a brief glimpse of the great unknown. It gave us a sneak peek into a world that cannot be seen. I'm talking about the spiritual realm. This used to creep me out simply because I didn't know much about it, and quite frankly, didn't care to. Oh, don't get me wrong. I loved reading about Heaven and how insanely awesome eternity will be for believers. It was the rest of the spiritual realm from which I steered clear. You know...the parts with evil spirits and demons and Hell.

This was not the sort of stuff I wanted to fill my mind with. And to be honest with you, I don't dwell on it a lot these days, either. Sure, I know it's there. I try to avoid pitfalls that may bring me any closer to these things, but I don't really give it any more credence than that. But whether I want to think about it or not, the Bible makes it clear that a spiritual realm exists. This fact was made eerily clear to me when I read Mark 5: 1 – 20 as a child.

> *[1] Jesus and his followers went to the other side of the lake to the area of the Gerasene[a] people. [2] When Jesus got out of the boat, instantly a man with an evil spirit came to him from the burial caves. [3] This man lived in the caves, and no one could tie him up, not even with a chain. [4] Many times people had used chains to tie the man's hands and feet, but he always broke them off. No one was strong enough to control him. [5] Day and night he would wander around the burial caves and on the hills, screaming and cutting himself with stones. [6] While Jesus was still far away, the man saw him, ran to him, and fell down before him. [7] The man shouted in a loud voice, "What do you want with me, Jesus, Son of the Most High God? I command you in God's name not to torture me!" [8] He said this because Jesus was saying to him, "You evil spirit, come out of the man." [9] Then Jesus asked him, "What is your name?" He answered, "My name is Legion,[b] because we are many spirits." [10] He begged Jesus again and again not to send them out of that area. [11] A large herd of pigs was feeding on a hill near there. [12] The demons begged Jesus, "Send us into the pigs; let us go into them." [13] So Jesus allowed them to do this. The evil spirits left the man and went into the pigs. Then the herd of pigs—about two thousand of them—rushed down*

the hill into the lake and were drowned. ¹⁴ The herdsmen ran away and went to the town and to the countryside, telling everyone about this. So people went out to see what had happened. ¹⁵ They came to Jesus and saw the man who used to have the many evil spirits, sitting, clothed, and in his right mind. And they were frightened. ¹⁶ The people who saw this told the others what had happened to the man who had the demons living in him, and they told about the pigs. ¹⁷ Then the people began to beg Jesus to leave their area. ¹⁸ As Jesus was getting back into the boat, the man who was freed from the demons begged to go with him. ¹⁹ But Jesus would not let him. He said, "Go home to your family and tell them how much the Lord has done for you and how he has had mercy on you." ²⁰ So the man left and began to tell the people in the Ten Towns[c] about what Jesus had done for him. And everyone was amazed.

So, there you have it. A mano-a-mano confrontation between Jesus and an evil spirit. Okay, I know *mano-a-mano* means *man to man* and that analogy doesn't fit here between the Son of God and a demon. But it sounds cool, so I'm keeping it for dramatic effect. This confrontation opened a whole other unearthly realm that I didn't want to think about when I read this as a child. But the more I read it as an adult, the more it moves up the charts as one of my all-time favorite stories. Let's break this meeting down a bit.

First, we should have a clear mental picture of the man who is filled with the evil spirit. He has all the appearances of a crazy person. Unshaven and filthy, sifting around rotting corpses in the burial caves. And if this, coupled with the fact that he was constantly screaming like a banshee and slicing himself open with jagged rocks wasn't enough to scare someone, check this out. The passage tells us *No one was strong enough to control him.* Sure, people had tried to contain him. Townsfolk had tried to chain him down, for his protection as well as their own. But chains couldn't hold him. He snapped the chains like they were paperclips. And he's about to have a showdown with the Prince of Peace.

This is going to be a confrontation of pure evil and pure righteousness. After reading the description of this demon-possessed man, you would think he would have no reservations about stepping up to the Son of God. And he doesn't. In fact, scripture tells us that once he saw Jesus, *he* approached *Him*. And he didn't just approach Him. He ran to Him. But it's what the man does next that really starts to veer this story in a different direction. He doesn't raise his fists to Christ. He doesn't even poke Him in the chest to try and instigate a fight. In my opinion, what he does next speaks more to this entire story than any other aspect of it. The man *fell down before Him.*

Immediately, the demon inside of this man not only knows who Jesus is, he knows the power that Jesus yields as well. So, he bows down before Him in subservient fashion. This is the same demon that mortal men could not control. He was used to having his way and not having to answer to anyone. But as soon as he saw Jesus, he ran to Him and bowed down. Let that sink in for a moment. Jesus is traveling the country, spreading the Gospel, and offering hope to everyone who will listen. And people who either heard Jesus speak or simply heard about Him had two choices. They could accept the fact that He is truly the Son of God, or they could choose to not believe. It's no different today. Some folks are sure that Christ is our savior. Some are convinced He is not. And others don't know and don't care. But this demon knew beyond a shadow of a doubt who Jesus was. And he was scared.

I say he was scared because of the dialogue that we read in this passage. Notice how he addresses Christ. *"What do you want with me, Jesus, Son of God Most High?"* He could have stopped with *"Jesus,"* but he doesn't. He goes on to show Jesus respect by acknowledging that he knows who He is as well as who sent Him. And I love the rest of the exchange as well. I'm paraphrasing here, but as Jesus commands the demon out of the man, the demon basically says, *"Okay...just don't hurt me. I'm asking this in God's name."* Now I wonder if that was a first in history. The first time a demon asked for something in God's name. But the fact that he tried speaks volumes not only to how scared he was but also how desperate he was.

And why? Jesus was one person. We find out that the demon's name is Legion because he is made up of many evil spirits. In fact, in those days, the Roman army's definition of a legion was five thousand men. So, based on that, we can assume that there were possibly that many evil spirits making up the demon. Five thousand evil spirits versus one man! And the spirits are running scared. That's the power that Jesus possesses. It could have been five *million* evil spirits, and the outcome would have been the same. They would have begged for mercy from the one man.

Here Jesus was, working to build a reputation in the world. He was sharing the path to salvation with everyone who would listen. He was performing miracles. He was healing the sick. Giving sight to the blind. Even raising the dead. Yet, many remained indifferent to him. And many others denied him. Yet, in the spiritual realm, inhabited by angels and demons, everyone knew who Jesus was…and they showed the appropriate respect.

That's the power that comes from Christ. If you're looking for more evidence, check out Luke, Chapter 4. Even when the devil tries to tempt Christ, all he can do is try to persuade Him. He knows he can't lay a finger on Jesus. That's the unadulterated power that He has. And that's the same protection He offers to each and every one of us. Yes, I used to be scared of this passage and the whole spiritual world it gives us a glimpse of. Now, I read it as one of my anchor passages, showing the frightening power that Jesus has. And the unmatched authority that he extends to every one of us as His children. He uses this influence as a blanket securing us all and keeping us from harm.

I also love this because it shows another level of Jesus' humility. Except for a time when He turned over a few tables in a temple, we never really see Jesus flex His muscles. More often than that, we see Him talking about forgiving your enemies or spreading peace. And that, my friends, is true power. He doesn't have to tell people what He can do if He gets annoyed. It's not like the Hulk and his catchphrase, *"Don't make me angry. You wouldn't like me when I'm angry."* Jesus preaches peace, but those who truly know Him, know His undeniable power. Luke 10:17 – 20 really drives the point home.

> *¹⁷ When the seventy-two came back, they were very happy and said, "Lord, even the demons obeyed us when we used your name!" ¹⁸ Jesus said, "I saw Satan fall like lightning from heaven. ¹⁹ Listen, I have given you power to walk on snakes and scorpions, power that is greater than the enemy has. So nothing will hurt you. ²⁰ But you should not be happy because the spirits obey you but because your names are written in heaven."*

Yes, I believe a Spiritual world exists. No, it doesn't frighten me anymore. Because with all the supernatural power that accompanies this realm, I know that I'm plugged into the most powerful source of all. It's a power source that will never run out or be depleted no matter how much I use it. And I thank Jesus for that every day.

One final thought about this passage that I feel is worth mentioning is the end. Did you catch the part where the man who was now free of the demons wanted to go with Jesus? In fact, he *begged* Him to take him along. Am I the only one who finds this a bit odd? We learn that he has a family back home that he probably hasn't seen in a while. Yet, he chooses to stay with Jesus. But, like all these stories, the more I read this one, the more it makes sense to me. Jesus changed this man's life. Not only did he change the man's life, He *saved* the man's life. And the man wanted more. He didn't want to see Jesus leave.

And that's what happens when we let Christ in. He changes us. Inwardly and outwardly. It's impossible to stay the same once Jesus comes into our hearts. And what happens next? We get greedy for it! We get greedy for Him! Greedy in a good way.

And we want more. That's all this man was doing. He wanted more of Jesus in his life. He probably just hadn't realized yet that once we accept Him into our lives, He dwells there forever. And so does His supernatural power.

Discussion Questions

1. When confronting the demon, Jesus' reputation preceded Him. The demon knew who He was and what He stood for. Does your reputation precede you? Are you demonstrative in your faith? Do others in your life know where you stand with Christ?

2. Do you truly believe that Jesus can change your life? Do you believe His power is just as strong today as it was when He walked the earth? Why or why not?

3. How do you think the story of Jesus and the demon fits into the Grand Narrative?

CHAPTER 6

A Serpent's Ceaseless Seduction
A Story of Adam and Eve

Since we've already discussed one talking animal in this book, let me backtrack to the opening book in the Bible and share the story of another one with you. You're probably a bit more familiar with this one. Here we find the story of Adam and Eve, the first humans God created. They lived in a perfect place called the Garden of Eden. Life was good. All their needs were met. God was with them and provided for them. The only rule God had for Adam and Eve was not to eat fruit from a specific tree that was located in the middle of the garden. This was the tree that gave the knowledge of good and evil. This perfect existence lasts for two whole chapters in the Bible. Then everything changes. Genesis 3:1 – 6 shows us why.

> *[1] Now the snake was the most clever of all the wild animals the Lord God had made. One day the snake said*

to the woman, "Did God really say that you must not eat fruit from any tree in the garden?" ² The woman answered the snake, "We may eat fruit from the trees in the garden. ³ But God told us, 'You must not eat fruit from the tree that is in the middle of the garden. You must not even touch it, or you will die.'" ⁴ But the snake said to the woman, "You will not die. ⁵ God knows that if you eat the fruit from that tree, you will learn about good and evil and you will be like God!" ⁶ The woman saw that the tree was beautiful, that its fruit was good to eat, and that it would make her wise. So she took some of its fruit and ate it. She also gave some of the fruit to her husband who was with her, and he ate it.

I know this sounds arrogant and self-righteous, but I can honestly say that I would not make the same mistake that Adam and Eve made. Am I smarter than them? Am I not influenced as easily? Am I an all-around better person than either of them was? No, no, and no. The reason I wouldn't have made the same mistake as them is that I am deathly afraid of snakes. One sight of the serpent and I would be history. Imagine the cartoon character that takes off running with blinding speed leaving a cloud of dust behind. That would be me! The snake wouldn't have been able to deliver his opening statement. I would have been gone!

Which brings me to my next argument as to why I wouldn't have made this same mistake. Simply put…it's a talking snake! First, it would take me a while to believe a snake was actually speaking. Secondly, it would take even longer for me to deem what the snake has to say as reliable! How gullible did Adam and Eve have to be to believe what the snake had to tell them? For years, this boggled my mind and lowered my opinion of the couple.

Then, one day as I was reading this story again, I saw it (and them) in a new light. Adam and Eve had taken some bad advice from an unlikely source, plain and simple. How many times has this same scenario played out in my life? Not via a talking snake, thank goodness, but it's happened, nonetheless. How many times have I listened to advice from someone I thought was a friend with my best interests at heart, even though deep down I knew better? How many times have I been negatively influenced by TV or movies, by the news, or by social media? Whether we like to admit it or not, we all live with some sort of talking snake in our lives. He's always trying to lead us down dark paths by showing us shortcuts or better yet, things we *deserve*.

That's usually how it starts. We're shown how we were wronged in some fashion and why we deserve what's coming to us, no matter how we get it. The snake's voice helps us to reason and rationalize our actions so that the end justifies the means and not vice versa. Facts get twisted and morals become distorted until we compromise our values and give the snake exactly what he wanted all along…obedience.

I can give you a real-life example of how I was almost a victim of this a while back. Being self-employed, I pay taxes and file reports on a monthly and quarterly basis. I've been doing this for decades. With the help of my accounting firm, I always file on time and according to federal and state guidelines. A few years back was no exception. Except for the fact that shortly after my quarterly report was mailed, I received a letter from the IRS stating that my report was never received and that they expected a prompt payment of a $100.00 late fee with a written explanation as to why this happened.

Now I know it sounds shady to say it was *lost in the mail.* But in this case, it was the truth. And I was hoping that years upon years of on-time reports and payments would buy me some grace. Or at least some credibility. It did not. They wouldn't even discuss the matter with me. There would be no negotiation or mediation. The IRS made it clear that they wanted my money, and they wanted my explanation. In that order. Needless to say, this did not sit well with me. And there was the opening the snake in my life needed. He started to whisper in my ear and gave me not only a sense of being victimized by the IRS but also a spirit of retribution. What could I do to make this situation right? This is *my* money that they are unfairly taking from me. How do I get back at them?

I decided that if they wanted to play hardball and take an additional $100.00 from me, I would simply not declare taxes on the next hundred or so books that I sold, just so I could pay myself back from the money they *stole* from me. I knew this act would be as immoral as it is illegal, but I didn't care. My actions were justified because of the unfair treatment I had suffered. They *owed* me this money and I was going to collect!

In my mind, for a short time, I not only listened to the snake in my life, but I started to conspire and collaborate with him. He assisted me in putting on my blinders and they helped block out any logic, common sense, or decency. Thank goodness for the family and friends in my life. They're the ones who help keep me grounded when I try and catch a train to *Crazy Town*. In the end, I paid the IRS their late fee and wrote an explanation, and

I went ahead and declared taxes on the other books I sold. And I'm not just saying that in case an IRS agent happens to read this book. I did it because it was the right thing to do. Do I agree with the way the IRS handled the situation? No. But that's *their* role. And as long as I'm an American citizen, it's *my* role to stay in compliance with them.

But for a brief time, the snake had me thinking differently. That's what he does. He waits for the opportunity to present himself and then strikes while the iron's hot. He takes black-and-white situations in our lives and mixes them into a beautiful shade of grey. And we start to question what's right and what's wrong. We start letting our ego drive our decisions. We feel we're owed something more than what we have. That's why it's so nice, and I believe necessary, to have a strong system of checks and balances in our lives. I feel the best system is that of our family and friends. The ones who truly love us and care about our well-being keep us grounded and on the right paths in life.

I sometimes wonder if that wasn't part of the problem with Adam and Eve. They didn't have any additional family at the time to help them rationalize their decision. Had they had a few more varying viewpoints over the forbidden fruit, maybe they would have said, *"Thanks, but no thanks,"* and our lives would be a lot different than they are today.

But life is what it is. It's wonderful, scary, remarkable, tragic, inspiring and deceiving. And just like Adam and Eve, we all have our own snakes in our own gardens to watch out for. It's not a matter of whether they will talk to us or not. It's a matter of whether we will listen.

Discussion Questions

1. Are there any *snakes in your garden* that are trying to speak to you? Are you listening? How can you distance yourself from these voices?

2. Do you have people in your life you can talk to about these temptations? Do you have a favorite Bible verse that helps keep you grounded?

3. How do you think the story of Adam and Eve fits into the Grand Narrative?

CHAPTER 7

More Malchus Please
A Story of Jesus

The next story I'd like to share with you is one that didn't necessarily scare me or confuse me. It didn't leave me scratching my head with a dumb look on my face when I finished reading it. (Okay, to be fair, the dumb look on my face is always there). This brief passage in the Bible simply left me wanting more. A character is introduced ever so briefly, has an encounter with Jesus, and is changed. That's how Jesus rolls, you know. Once you experience him, it's impossible to stay the same person you were before. The Bible is full of stories of folks who have experienced Christ's love, mercy, and power. We don't know what happened to each one of these characters, so why should this one be any different? The reason is simple. This character wasn't someone who came looking for Jesus in the same way so many others had up to this point. He wasn't looking for a miracle or hoping to hear Him speak. He had come with the crowd to arrest Jesus.

First, there is the confrontation. Then comes the gratuitous violence. Followed by the supernatural. Then...nothing. We don't know what becomes of this man. Here is the actual story from Luke 22 to which I'm referring:

> *⁴⁷ While Jesus was speaking, a crowd came up, and Judas, one of the twelve apostles, was leading them. He came close to Jesus so he could kiss him. ⁴⁸ But Jesus said to him, "Judas, are you using the kiss to give the Son of Man to his enemies?" ⁴⁹ When those who were standing around him saw what was happening, they said, "Lord, should we strike them with our swords?" ⁵⁰ And one of them struck the servant of the high priest and cut off his right ear. ⁵¹ Jesus said, "Stop! No more of this." Then he touched the servant's ear and healed him. ⁵² Those who came to arrest Jesus were the leading priests, the soldiers who guarded the Temple, and the elders. Jesus said to them, "You came out here with swords and clubs as though I were a criminal. ⁵³ I was with you every day in the Temple, and you didn't arrest me there. But this is your time—the time when darkness rules."*

Picture this scene. The mob is coming to arrest Jesus. One of His followers, (the Book of John suggests it was Simon Peter), whips out his sword, yells *"Not on my watch!"* and slices off the right ear of the high priest's servant. Before this blows into a full-fledged riot, Jesus calms the crowd and heals the servant's ear. I don't know if Jesus touched the side of his head and another ear grew back or if He bent down and picked up the freshly sliced ear and miraculously reattached it. But what we do know is that Jesus healed him with a simple touch.

What makes this passage so interesting to me is that I want to know the rest of this servant of the high priest's story. What happens next? The way I see it is this. After what this momentarily earless man, (The Book of John tells us his name is Malchus), has just experienced, he has two choices. He can believe that the man they just arrested is truly the Son of God and they have just made a huge mistake. Or he can chalk up what just happened to some sort of magic trick and continue to believe that Jesus is a blasphemous criminal who deserves to be locked up and have the key thrown away. His choice always reminds me of the famous Albert Einstein quote, *"There are two ways to live: you can live as if nothing is a miracle; you can live as if everything is a miracle."*

So, what *does* the next chapter of Malchus' life have in store? What did he truly take away from that experience? This is one of the first questions I have once I get to Heaven. Maybe it's the writer in me, but I hate open endings. I need to know *what happens next!* This is probably part of the reason that I still watch professional wrestling. It may explain why I never used to miss an episode of *Day of Our Lives*. And it may reveal some truth as to why I still pick up a comic book to read on occasion. It's because all three of these outlets have one major theme in common. They're all continuing stories. They've been told for decades. Characters change, but the stories continue. And I want to know what happens next!

Wanting some closure on this issue is part of the reason that this passage fascinates me. But the reason this story, or lack thereof, interests me, is that Malchus is a microcosm of a broader theme of Jesus in our lives. Do we accept Him and all that He does for us? Or do we let cynicism creep in and find reasons to doubt Him or what He can do? Going back to the Einstein quote from earlier, I choose to look at life as if everything is a miracle, simply because this is what I believe. Every breath you take, every move you make (admit it…you just sang that last line, didn't you?), everything surrounding us, these are all nothing short of miracles.

And these miracles are gifts from God. And as with any gift, we can choose to accept or reject what He has for us. Choosing to see or not to see. Determining to accept or to reject. Deciding to believe or to doubt. It all comes down to choice. As a believer, I feel this is yet another gift He has given us. God doesn't force us to bow down and worship Him. If this was His plan, I doubt He would have given us the gift of free will. He wants us to choose Him. He longs for us to come willingly to Him. And He's waiting with open arms. But again, the choice is ours. The beginning of Matthew 27:2 sums this choice up perfectly when Pilate poses this question to the angry crowds that have gathered to hear what Christ's fate will be.

> *Pilate asked, "So what should I do with Jesus, the one called the Christ?"*

Isn't that the ultimate question for us all? What do we do with Jesus, the one called the Christ? It's a question that we must all answer eventually. Are we going to ignore Him? Are we going to believe, but keep Him at arms-length? Are we going to treat him like a great-great-great-great-grandfather in a nursing home and stop in and say "hi" to Him every Sunday and then put Him out of our minds again as soon as we leave? Or are we going to embrace Him? Are we going to let Him into our lives and allow Him to radically change us? Are we going to trust Him unconditionally? Are we going to try and transform our lives to be more like His?

The choice is ours. And I honestly believe that God will respect whatever decision we make. One decision will change our hearts while another one will break His. One decision will allow God to use us for greater purposes than we could ever imagine. And another decision will keep us firmly planted where we are now.

We can see, but not believe. We can sense, but try to rationalize. We can feel, but just ignore. I don't know what road Malchus chose. As I said earlier, it's one of my many questions for when I get to Heaven, and I hope I get to ask Malchus himself. Although, I guess if he's there, the question is already answered. The bottom line is this; he had a choice to make. And he made one. Each of us has a choice to make. If you've chosen to accept Christ into your life and recognize the miracles all around you each day, then you know how fulfilling the life He intended for you to have can be. If you're still on the fence about Jesus and what He's all about, my advice to you is this. Talk to him about it. Jesus never says, *"Make the choice to accept me, and then we'll talk."* He loves each and every one of us as if we were his one and only child. And wherever you are on your spiritual path, Jesus would love for you to check in with Him.

How we choose to deal with Jesus is our decision to make. But He's already let us know how He chooses to deal with us… with unconditional, unadulterated love.

Discussion Questions

1. How do you view the wonders of the world? Are they mundane or miraculous?

2. Just like Pilate's question, what will *you* do with the one called the Christ? Will you choose to trust Christ with every aspect of your life? Or will you keep Him at arms-length? Why or why not?

3. How do you think the story of Malchus fits into the Grand Narrative?

CHAPTER 8

Snake Handling 101
A Story of Moses

While this book is mostly about stories from the Bible that scared me, I would be a bit remiss if I didn't also throw in my number one fear of all time…snakes! I know we covered a talking snake earlier in this book when we visited the Garden of Eden, but I'm referring to the fear of actually (I just shuddered even thinking about the word) *touching* a snake. Naturally a Bible story about just that had to make the book. So here we go. Read Exodus 4:1-5.

> *[1] Then Moses answered, "What if the people of Israel do not believe me or listen to me? What if they say, 'The Lord did not appear to you'?" [2] The Lord said to him, "What is that in your hand?" Moses answered, "It is my walking stick." [3] The Lord said, "Throw it on the ground." So Moses threw it on the ground, and it became a snake. Moses ran from the snake, [4] but the Lord said to him, "Reach out and grab the snake by its tail." When Moses*

reached out and took hold of the snake, it again became a stick in his hand. ⁵ *The Lord said, "This is so that the Israelites will believe that the Lord appeared to you. I am the God of their ancestors, the God of Abraham, the God of Isaac, and the God of Jacob."*

The backstory to this dialogue between Moses and God is as follows. God has chosen Moses to lead His people out of Egypt to freedom. Moses is a little more than hesitant to accept this position, so God is showing him different miracles that He will allow him to perform. This will help prove to the Israelites that he was chosen by God and that this break from the tyranny of the Egyptians is His will.

For a moment, please allow me to dwell on the superficiality of the story. Actually touching a slithering snake. In the passage we just read, God tells Moses to pick up the snake...*BY ITS TAIL!!!* Anyone who knows anything about snakes knows that, unless you are an experienced snake handler, this is *NOT* the way to pick up a snake. The proper way is to pick one up right behind its head, as close to the jawbone as possible. Grabbing the snake anywhere else is usually a precursor for it to revert to defense mode and strike at its handler.

I learned this the hard way when I was a college student. I was living in a house with four other guys and one of them decided to buy a ball python as a pet. Yes, he knew my unhealthy fear of snakes. And no, decades later, I have still not forgiven him. One weekend, all my roommates traveled to their respective homes and left me by myself to hold down the fort. I know what you're thinking...the snake escaped, and I had a horrific run-in with it. No. Nothing as cliché as that.

The snake's owner called me from home, a convenient two hundred miles away, to let me know that Sid (yes, the snake's name was Sid) was sick and taking antibiotics. He had *forgotten* to share this information with me before he left but was now in dire straits. Someone had to administer Sid's medicine to him, and I was his last resort. And this wasn't a matter of just throwing a pill into his tank and hoping he mistook it for a rat. I had to pour the antibiotic into a syringe and give the snake a shot. I knew from watching others that Sid didn't particularly like to be handled. I could only imagine how much he would enjoy being stabbed with a needle. I called a mutual friend of my roommate's and mine to come over and assist with the procedure. It took every ounce of courage I could muster, but I was finally able to reach my hand into the tank to pick up Sid. In my infinite wisdom, I decided it would be best to keep my hand as far away from his mouth as possible, so I gently cupped his underbelly about midway down the four-foot physique.

What happened next is very predictable. The snake took exception to being manhandled and, faster than anything I've ever seen in my life, struck back at my exposed arm. To Sid's credit, he didn't bite me. But he was securely wrapped around my forearm, cutting off circulation to my hand and staring at me with a look that communicated, *"Think very carefully about your next move."* My hand was already turning a bright shade of purple by the time our friend pried Sid off me, handling him the correct way, I might add. So, what was the point of this trip down memory lane? It was my long, drawn-out way of saying that I know first-hand how dangerous it is to pick up a snake by its tail. And living through this experience only compounded my fear of snakes.

It's the old *if/then* scenario. *If* you pick a snake up by its tail, *then* you are more than likely going to suffer the consequences. So why did God give *these* specific instructions? My theory is this. Most anyone could distract a snake with one hand and then swoop in and pick it up by the back of the neck with his other. Where would the trust in that be? By picking the snake up by the tail, Moses was living his faith by essentially saying, *"God, this makes no worldly sense, but You've called me to do this and I'm trusting You."*

I know that some purists would say that may not be the case and that this was simply a miraculous demonstration that God was passing down to Moses to use to convince his fellow Israelites. But for any good plan to succeed, there must be an element of trust between the leader and the followers. Yes, this was something God was passing on to Moses as a tool, but it was also a demonstration of trust. Moses had to be able to trust in God to carry out His plans for the nation.

When I was younger, it was the actual handling of the snake that scared me the most in this passage. As time passed, what started to scare me more than the snake, was the thought of God asking me to pick one up by its tail. For a long time, if you were to ask me, *"Do you trust God?"*, the answer would have been a boastful, emphatic *"YES! I'm a champion for Christ! Of course I do!"* If you were to ask me, *"Do you trust God enough to pick a snake up by the tail if He asked you?"* there would have been a moment of hesitation before I responded with a small, somewhat inaudible, *"yeah...sure...whatever."* And that was the rub of it. For as much as I claimed to have accepted Jesus into my heart and for as much as I talked about keeping Him first in my life, I had a hard time answering this question. Would I be able to face a fear that God brought to me?

Then I looked back on my life and discovered some key moments where God had already asked me to *pick a snake up by the tail*. The one that sticks out in my mind is when God called me to start speaking in public. Now we all know that the fear of public speaking is common. In fact, it ranks higher than the fear of snakes for most Americans. But did you know that in several opinion polls, the fear of public speaking outranks the fear of death? Some people would rather *die* than speak in front of a crowd. The fear of snakes still comes in at number one as far as my fears are concerned, but public speaking isn't far behind.

And much like my fear of picking up snakes, my fear of public speaking was justified. You see, I failed public speaking in college not once, but twice. I switched majors so that I never had to take public speaking a third time. By this point, I felt like I was living out the definition of insanity. I was doing the same thing, (taking the same class) over and over, but expecting different results. I switched from a criminal justice major to a psychology major based on this fact alone. So, you can imagine my reluctance when God started presenting me with speaking opportunities later in my life. I declined as many as I could before realizing that His hand may be at work in this. When I finally took this issue to Him in prayer, I reminded Him of not only how badly speaking to large groups frightened me, but also to check my transcripts from the 1990s to see just how horrible I was at this kind of thing.

Soon after that, God directed me to a passage I had read dozens of times but never given a second thought. I now recite it before every speech I give or class I teach. It's Deuteronomy 31:6.

Be strong and brave. Don't be afraid of them and don't be frightened, because the Lord your God will go with you. He will not leave you or forget you.

Here, Moses is talking to the Israelites right before he turns the reigns over to Joshua, describing their trek into the Promised Land. But God was showing me that these words were equally applicable to the journey to which He was calling me. Today, speaking and teaching are two of the most enjoyable aspects of my job. Just like Moses and the snake, God took one of my biggest, most justifiable fears and turned it into one of my greatest joys. Only God is capable of a miracle like this. And just like He commanded Moses, it only happens when we trust God and grab with reckless abandon what scares us the most.

Discussion Questions

1. Are there any *snakes* in your life that God is encouraging you to grab by the tail? Are there any areas of your life where you need to replace fear with faith?

2. Can you remember a time when you trusted God even though a consequence appeared predetermined, but He changed the outcome?

3. How do you think the story of Moses and the snake fits into the Grand Narrative?

CHAPTER 9

May I Follow?
A Story of Jesus

Before we move on to any new stories, I'd like to revisit one we've already covered. Turn with me if you would back to Mark, chapter 5. Remember the showdown between Jesus and the demon named Legion? There was still always one part of that story that troubled me. Yes, the demon was vanquished. Yes, good prevailed over evil. Yes, Jesus once again showed just how cool He is. But the ending of this passage left me a little puzzled. Read the last few verses one more time.

> *[18] As Jesus was getting back into the boat, the man who was freed from the demons begged to go with him. [19] But Jesus would not let him. He said, "Go home to your family and tell them how much the Lord has done for you and how he has had mercy on you." [20] So the man left and began to tell the people in the Ten Towns about what Jesus had done for him. And everyone was amazed.*

Jesus wouldn't let him come with them? What is this all about? This is the same Jesus who's traveling all over the countryside trying to convert folks to follow Him. Isn't this move somewhat contradictory? We only have to backtrack a few chapters in Mark to find Jesus literally calling others to follow Him. Mark 1:16-20 paints a pretty clear picture.

[16] When Jesus was walking by Lake Galilee, he saw Simon and his brother Andrew throwing a net into the lake because they were fishermen. [17] Jesus said to them, "Come follow me, and I will make you fish for people." [18] So Simon and Andrew immediately left their nets and followed him. [19] Going a little farther, Jesus saw two more brothers, James and John, the sons of Zebedee. They were in a boat, mending their nets. [20] Jesus immediately called them, and they left their father in the boat with the hired workers and followed Jesus.

And let's not forget about the rich young ruler that Jesus counseled. When asked what it would take to have eternal life, Jesus entered into this exchange with him in Matthew 19:17-22.

[17] Jesus answered, "Why do you ask me about what is good? Only God is good. But if you want to have life forever, obey the commands." [18] The man asked, "Which commands?" Jesus answered, "'You must not murder anyone; you must not be guilty of adultery; you must not steal; you must not tell lies about your neighbor; [19] honor your father and mother;[a] and love your neighbor as you

love yourself.'" [20] *The young man said, "I have obeyed all these things. What else do I need to do?"* [21] *Jesus answered, "If you want to be perfect, then go and sell your possessions and give the money to the poor. If you do this, you will have treasure in heaven. Then come and follow me."* [22] *But when the young man heard this, he left sorrowfully, because he was rich.*

I know there's a lot to digest there but check out Jesus' last line. *"Then come and follow me."* This command is all over the pages of the Bible. Jesus seems to always be telling folks to follow Him. He called the original disciples. Then we have the guy who wanted to go bury his father (a reasonable request, I thought) in Matthew 8:22. Then there's Matthew the Tax Collector in Matthew 9:9. In fact, in each of the Gospels, we find Jesus gathering followers. And the exclamation point on all of this can be found in John 12:26. Jesus clearly states that,

Whoever serves me must follow me. Then my servant will be with me everywhere I am. My Father will honor anyone who serves me.

So, with all these examples, why in the world would Jesus clearly tell the new and improved demon-free gentleman specifically *not* to follow Him? Is this another of the Bible's contradictions that some people like to call out? Did this former demon-possessed guy do something to excommunicate himself? Was he not likeable? Was he a close talker? Did he have bad breath? Did he chew with his mouth open? Did he finish other people's sentences? What was it?

It was none of the above. Jesus didn't allow him to follow because He needed him exactly where he was. In fact, just like good leaders do, Jesus even told him *why* he didn't want him to follow.

> *"Go home to your family and tell them how much the Lord has done for you and how he has had mercy on you."*

Jesus had plans for this man. This is no different from what we covered in the last chapter regarding God having plans for our lives. Christianity is a very personal religion. It involves a special intimacy between us and Christ. We are all blessed with spiritual gifts and called to use them in specific ways. At specific times. In specific places.

When it's all said and done, following Jesus is not a geographical call. It's a Spiritual call. We can follow Him and serve Him anytime and anywhere. This reminds me of a situation I found myself in a few years ago. I submitted a proposal to speak at a conference. I felt this would be a great way to share God's message in front of a large audience and I would definitely be *following* Him, using the gifts He had blessed me with. Long story short, my proposal was shot down in a blaze of glory. Very humiliating. And my first reaction? Well God, if you don't want to use me here, I'll just go do something else. Years later, this is still embarrassing to admit. My immaturity was so rampant that I decided to take my proverbial ball and go home. *I tried, God. If you want to close this door, oh well. I'll just take my bitterness and head off in a completely different direction.* My reaction should have been prayer. *God, what do you want me to learn from this?* Or, *God, thank you for closing this door. I trust your wisdom.* Or, *God, does this rejection position me for something different you have in mind?*

It turns out that the latter was true. The panel that had dismissed my proposal reached back out to me to see if they could contract me to help train future keynote speakers. Now, instead of influencing one audience, God was positioning me to help several other speakers influence hundreds of audiences going forward. He showed me that I don't always need the spotlight to follow Him. I just have to be willing to zig with His zag. To adjust my schedule to His. To be open to opportunities I would never imagine.

The older I get, the more I've come to realize that following Jesus is scary and exciting at the same time. And His plans often deviate from mine. But I've learned that some of my best times and some of my most successful ventures have come from when my initial plans failed, sometimes in glorious fashion. But I remained open to His call. I hope you choose to follow Jesus. Whatever that looks like in your life. Wherever that takes you in your life. When we follow Jesus, we're always on the right path.

Discussion Questions

1. Have you chosen to follow Jesus? If not, why not? If yes, what does this look like in your life?

2. Do you believe that God can use you to carry out His will, despite your past? Do you believe He *does* use you to carry out His will, despite your past?

3. How do you think this story of Jesus fits into the Grand Narrative?

CHAPTER 10

What's in a Name?
A Story of Lot's Wife

This next story is one that frightened me and confused me on multiple levels when I read it in my youth. It's the story of a man named Lot and his getaway from the city of Sodom. You've probably heard of Sodom, usually listed with its sister city of Gomorrah. Both were bad places. You've heard the term, *A nice place to visit, but you wouldn't want to live there?* From what the Bible tells us about these places, you wouldn't even want to stop in and ask for directions. I won't go into detail about Sodom, but it was so terrible that God declared that it and all its inhabitants were worth destroying. However, He waits until a few of His angels escort Lot and his family out of the danger zone first. But as we soon find out, they're not all completely safe. Here's exactly how it goes down in Genesis 19:23-26.

[23] The sun had already come up when Lot entered Zoar. [24] The Lord sent a rain of burning sulfur down from the sky on Sodom and Gomorrah [25] and destroyed those cities.

> *He also destroyed the whole Jordan Valley, everyone living in the cities, and even all the plants. ²⁶ At that point Lot's wife looked back. When she did, she became a pillar of salt.*

The two issues I wrestled with were these: 1. Did God really just kill someone for turning her head? And 2. Why a pillar of salt? I'm not trying to trivialize this story. These were real questions I had about this passage, and nobody ever seemed like they wanted to explain it in further detail. When I would press my Sunday School teachers, I would get answers such as, *"Let's just concentrate on what happens to Lot next,"* or *"You're making too much out of this. If she were that important, the Bible would have given her a name,"* or *"I can't take your questions seriously while you're wearing that white Don Johnson jacket and skinny black leather tie."* Which, for the record, looked good at the time. I had the look of Sonny Crockett, but unfortunately, the coolness of Rico Tubbs.

Let's start with the first question. *Did God really just kill someone for turning her head?* Obviously, the answer is yes. But in fairness, she was given specific instructions to not do that very thing. Earlier in the chapter, one of the angels tells them this:

> *Run for your lives! Don't look back or stop anywhere in the valley. Run to the mountains, or you will be destroyed.*

She was warned. She didn't listen. She was killed. So, does the punishment fit the crime here? It seems a little harsh, but that's not for me to judge. What was the point of this penalty? Its story made it into the pages of the Bible, so there must be something we can learn from it. *Obey God or be punished for every misstep?* No. Thank goodness! If that were the case, we'd all be in trouble. Maybe, *Look to the Future and Never Look Back?* No. As much as God is interested in whom we are as opposed to whom we were, there are advantages to learning from our pasts.

I think the bigger lesson here is that her time on Earth was cut short and because of that, she was never able to become the person that God had intended her to be. We are introduced to Lot's wife in the Bible, and just like that, her character is taken away from us. We never even knew her name. Why is that? Almost every other character in the Bible is mentioned by name. Heck, a lot of them have more than one. Names were very important back in this day. Look how many books of the Bible include family lineages full of names. Names were a big deal! So why is Lot's wife's name curiously omitted?

Did God not love her as much as He did everyone else? No, that's not the case, either. The Lord's not known to play favorites. I think the story of Lot's wife is an admonitory tale for the rest of us. Lot's wife is the quintessential story of *what could have been.* God may have had huge plans for this woman. He may have chosen her to change the world. But we'll never know. She disobeyed God. And because of this, not only was her life cut short, but none of us will ever even know her name.

God calls on all of us all the time. He has plans for us. He tells us so in Psalm 40:5 and reminds us again in Jeremiah 29:11. And he doesn't rely on us for our ability but for our *availability.* Lot's wife did not make herself available to be used. And unlike most of us today, she had distinct and specific instructions of precisely what to do and not to do in this situation. And on top of all that, she was told exactly what would happen if she didn't comply.

You may think it's comparing apples to oranges to put Lot's wife's episode against Moses being called to lead God's people out of Egypt, Jonah being sent to Ninevah, or Noah being told to prepare for some bad weather. But I don't think so. All these examples fall under the same category of God calling on *someone* to do *something*. We're all part of His perfect plan. To carry out His will, He has always used people. And the beauty of this is, we don't have to be the smartest or the best looking or the most popular person to be chosen. In fact, God has a history of picking the least likely to succeed in carrying out His plans. That way, He gets the glory!

God still calls on us every day. It may not be a life-changing request like it was for Abraham or Moses. It may be so minuscule that we don't even notice it or connect it to being from God. Maybe it's God putting in your heart to smile at a stranger, hold the door for someone, or let someone merge in front of you in traffic. Perhaps it's telling your spouse he or she looks nice today. It may be spending more time with your kids. It could be giving up your seat on the bus for someone else to sit down. Whether it's big or small, we should answer God's call. That last line would make a great song lyric, wouldn't it? I need to copyright that before I forget.

When we obey God and listen to what He's saying to us, we may become better people. We may help others in need. We just might change the world. Philippians 1:6 tells us that,

God began doing a good work in you, and I am sure he will continue it until it is finished when Jesus Christ comes again.

God is always at work in our lives and all He asks for is our readiness. You've seen the ones in the Bible who gave theirs. And now you know one who did not. The names of the ones who listened to God are shared, and their stories are legendary. Lot's wife never used the opportunity she was given. And her story ends abruptly, and her name is not just forgotten. It was never even known.

So why a pillar of salt? A simple lightning bolt to smite her would have sufficed, right? Here are my thoughts on that. Turning into a pillar of salt was just one more reminder of what she could have been. In Matthew 5:13, Jesus tells us,

You are the salt of the earth. But if the salt loses its salty taste, it cannot be made salty again. It is good for nothing, except to be thrown out and walked on.

Webster's dictionary defines *Salt of the Earth* as "a very good and honest person or group of people." Jesus was complimenting those who follow Him, letting them know their value, and at the same time, warning them to guard their faith at all times.

Salt also adds flavor. And flavor, by definition, is a distinctive appealing or enlivening quality. An appealing or enlivening quality! These characteristics help with engagement and that's exactly where God wants us to be. Engaged with other people. That's why the Bible is so big on fellowship. Real change happens in groups. The more engaged we are, the more lives we can change, including our own!

That's why I think the pillar of salt is all that was left. Just one last memento of what could have been. But remember, God is in control. And He makes the best out of all circumstances. Lot's wife may not have gone on to make any grand contributions to the world she lived in way back when. But she serves as an example for us of what not to do when God gives us direction. God probably won't turn you or me into a pillar of salt the next time we ignore His voice or act in our own self-interest. But when we do this, we will never become the person God has called us to be. We will never accomplish the great things He has in mind for us. In John 14:12 Jesus says,

> *I tell you the truth, whoever believes in me will do the same things that I do. Those who believe will do even greater things than these, because I am going to the Father.*

The choice is ours. Do we want to make a difference in this world by listening for and obeying God's call? Or are we content to ignore the call, do our own thing, and risk never being remembered for anything? And while I may have made a big deal about names in this chapter, please remember this. I believe our names are important. But not as important as the only name that matters when all is said and done. The beautiful and powerful name of Jesus.

Discussion Questions

1. Are you ready to answer God's call? Pray about this. What may He be leading you toward? What may He be leading you away from?

2. Is what you're doing in life right now for your glory? Or for His? Are you working to honor your name? Or His?

3. How do you think the story of Lot's wife fits into the Grand Narrative?

CHAPTER 11

Biblical Oxymorons?
A Story of Isaiah and Matthew

One lesson I was taught over and over again as a child in Sunday School was that the Bible would never contradict itself. And through my childlike faith (which, again, I was taught over and over again to have), I believed that. So, you can imagine my fear and confusion when I compared Isaiah 1:17 to Matthew 5:39. Here are two verses that, on the surface, seem to be the antithesis of one another. This couldn't be, could it? If this were true, then my entire belief system was at risk. Everything I'd been taught and led to believe up to this point was in grave danger of unraveling. Pretty scary stuff for a young man.

What's that? You don't know Isaiah 1:17 and Matthew 5:39 by heart? You have no idea what I'm talking about yet? That's quite alright. Don't ever feel bad about not memorizing Bible verses. Outside of John 3:16, I can count the number of verses I can recite by memory on one hand. And still have fingers left over. Remember, it's better to understand the Bible than to memorize it. But that's a lesson for another time. Let's look at both verses in question, shall we? First, Isaiah 1:17:

Learn to do good. Seek justice. Punish those who hurt others. Help the orphans. Stand up for the rights of widows.

Talk about a verse you can really get behind! This one sounds like it was derived straight from the curriculum of *Becoming A Superhero 101*. It speaks to the inner champion in all of us, does it not? Do what's right. Look for fairness. Make those that offend others pay. And defend those who can't defend themselves. Even as I'm typing this, I'm sitting up a little taller in my chair. My muscles are slightly flexed. Part of me wants to run out into the street looking for a wrong to make right. That's the God-inspiring power of this verse. It encourages us. It emboldens us. It validates that the world is a scary place and that we have the power to go out and make it less frightening. I start each morning with a cup of coffee and a review of this verse.

Now let's visit Matthew 5:39.

But I tell you, don't stand up against an evil person. If someone slaps you on the right cheek, turn to him the other cheek also.

Okay, so this is where it got sticky for me. Isaiah built me up. And then Matthew came along and sucked all the wind out of my sails. Honestly, the first time I compared these two verses, I was content to paraphrase them as follows: Isaiah 1:17: *"Be a man."* Matthew 5:39: *"Be a wimp."* The Matthew verse did not sit well with me for years. And it bothered me even more because these words of nonviolence, these words of not sticking up for ourselves, they came from Jesus, Himself. He spoke them as He was teaching His disciples on a hillside one day. So here was my dilemma. These two verses seemed to be polar opposite positions on how to handle ourselves. Yet I knew that the Bible doesn't contradict itself. And I also knew that Jesus always spoke the truth. So where do I go from here?

The answer to that question is three-pronged and it is the same answer to most all my theological questions. I have three sources to tap into. They are God, the Bible, and other friends of faith. I took my question to the Lord in prayer. I read more of the Bible. Sometimes verses can be taken out of context. When we read the surrounding scripture or perhaps even the entire chapter, clarity often occurs. Finally, I talked with church friends I have who are much more knowledgeable than me and got their take on the matter.

All three of these venues spoke to me and gave me a higher level of clarity on the matter. It all comes down to perspective. Is what we do for ourselves or for others? Read Isaiah again. *Learn to do good. Seek justice. Punish those who hurt others. Help the orphans. Stand up for the rights of widows.* Study the verbs here. Learn. Seek. Punish. Stand up for. These are all external actions we can take that affect the world around us. Now notice the nouns. Good. Justice. Others. Orphans. Widows. This is nothing more than a compilation of what God wants us to pursue and for whom He wants us to pursue it.

Now, on to Matthew 5:39. To be fair, let's revisit it as well. *But I tell you, don't stand up against an evil person. If someone slaps you on the right cheek, turn to him the other cheek also.* Where is the perspective directed in this one? It's internal. In Isaiah, we were talking about what to do to help others. Here in Matthew, Jesus is telling us how to act when something is done directly to us. Jesus is telling us to love our enemies. He's teaching us tolerance and peace. We know our breaking points. We recognize our limits. We realize what we can tolerate and what we can't. And one slap to the cheek or one (insert infraction here) is typically bearable to us. I feel that Jesus is helping to build our character with this teaching. He's basically saying that most times, by taking the high road like this, the situation will diffuse itself. Other times, it may continue. When this happens, I don't think God is telling us to lie down and be a doormat for anyone. I think He just wants us to give spiritual maturity a chance before taking other actions.

It reminds me of a Patrick Swayze quote from his bouncer days in one of my favorite movies, *Roadhouse*. He simply tells his bouncer crew to *"Be nice. Until it's time to not be nice."*

"How are we going to know when that is?" asks one of his staff.

"You won't. I'll let you know," replies Swayze.

And I believe that's how God works. He wants us to practice what He preaches in Matthew. But we also have a limited number of cheeks to turn. When we follow God's word, He will always lead us in the right direction, and more importantly, show us what actions to take. Remember, we are always acting as ambassadors for Him. Don't think for a moment that He is going to leave us alone to fend for ourselves.

To sum up this chapter, the biggest distinction between the two verses is the fact of whether we are standing up to help others or standing up to protect our pride. Pride is not a bad thing, but it's a slippery slope. Too much of it can be a problem and God knows that about His creation. That's why I feel He commands us to be a lot more tolerant of wrongdoing against ourselves than against others. The second chapter in Philippians backs this up. Verses 3 and 4 say this:

> *³ When you do things, do not let selfishness or pride be your guide. Instead, be humble and give more honor to others than to yourselves. ⁴ Do not be interested only in your own life, but be interested in the lives of others."*

Simply stated…put others first. This reminds me of a story of when my kids were much younger. My daughter was in fourth grade and my son was in second. They went to the same school and rode the same bus together every day. My son came home one day and told me there was an older boy on the bus picking on him. I told Tyler to try ignoring the bully and hopefully the situation would resolve itself. If it didn't, then he was to stand up to the punk, excuse me…young man, and tell him enough was enough.

The bullying continued for another day or so and Tyler, more patient and tolerant at that age than I am today, simply ignored the behavior, and *poof,* like magic, it just disappeared. Fortunately for Tyler, the kid had picked a different victim now.

Unfortunately for him, it was my daughter and Tyler's sister, Kayla. The kid grabbed Kayla's backpack, threw it in the bus aisle, and started to laugh at her. The laughter didn't last long. Tyler grabbed the kid, threw him down, and said to him, *"Nobody messes with my sister!"* Okay, I may be guilty of letting him watch too many action movies from the 80s with me for him to pick up that kind of cheesy dialogue, but that's what happened. And a prouder dad I could not have been! Yes, Tyler got in trouble with the school. Yes, I was informed of the incident. Yes, Tyler had to sit in the front seat of the bus to and from school for the next month, but *no*...that kid never bullied anyone on that bus again.

Notice the stark contrast of Tyler's behavior that drives home the message of these Bible verses so well. When trouble came his way, he did what he could to tolerate it. He wasn't going to stay on this course forever, but he did at least give it a shot. And it paid off. When he saw trouble head toward someone he loved, he acted immediately. There was no discussion with dear old dad like the first time. He instantly got involved. And in each scenario, the message was sent and received. In this case, the kid realized there was no use in picking on Tyler because he was above this childish behavior. And he quickly realized there was no use picking on anyone else on the bus because Tyler wasn't going to condone that action.

I'm certainly not advocating for vigilante justice at the drop of a hat. In fact, the beauty of this is that both circumstances call for a level of maturity. This demonstrates balance in our lives. While we try to discipline ourselves to not let much rattle us personally, we should also discipline ourselves to stand up for others whenever we can, when the situation calls for it. So, there you have it. Another fear of mine alleviated. I still believe that the Bible never contradicts itself. Sometimes we just have to study the passages a little more closely. And I think that's part of God's perfect plan.

Discussion Questions

1. Who are the *orphans or widows* in your life that you could be helping? What are some specific ways you could serve them?

2. Is there anyone in your life you need to forgive? Is there anyone in your life you would like forgiveness from?

3. How do you think these verses fit into the Grand Narrative?

CHAPTER 12

Too Much Studying May Be Hazardous To Your Health
A Story of King Solomon

Just to shake things up, allow me to share a verse from the Bible that didn't actually scare me as a kid. But it is one that, as a teenager, I manipulated for my own personal gain before I really knew what it meant. It is Ecclesiastes 12:12 and it states,

So be careful, my son, about other teachings. People are always writing books, and too much study will make you tired.

You can imagine how I used this line, right? Whenever my parents would tell me it was time to quit watching *He-Man* cartoons and start doing homework, I would conveniently and nonchalantly drop some Ecclesiastes on them. Now, my parents were God-fearing folks, but they weren't stupid. They knew I was taking this verse out of context and this stunt would buy me maybe 15 minutes tops. But hey, that was sometimes all I needed to see He-Man lay the smackdown on Skeletor one more time.

I can't remember how I even stumbled upon this verse. It's not one of the most popular ones. I doubt you'll see this one as a bumper sticker on the car in front of you in traffic or have this printed on your favorite coffee mug. Like a lot of the verses we've covered, I really didn't think about this obscure line from Ecclesiastes until I started writing this book. And God laid it on my heart to examine it further. I guess He figured since I had abused this passage in my younger years, the least I could do was study it and share my findings today. Which is exactly what I'm going to do.

First, let's look at who wrote the book of Ecclesiastes. Most believe it was King Solomon. One of the wisest men to ever walk the earth. Which in retrospect, I should have used this fact to back up this verse to my parents when I was younger. Who knows? That may have bought me another five minutes of TV. Anyway, where was I? Oh yeah, Solomon was a wise dude. Solomon asked God for wisdom and God responded. I Kings 3:12 shares this.

I will do what you asked. I will give you wisdom and understanding that is greater than anyone has had in the past or will have in the future.

So, if Solomon included this little nugget of wisdom in scripture, surely it has relevance to us. My take on this? In its most simplistic form? Reading and studying are great. I believe they're both integral to leading a successful and influential life.

But the point I feel Solomon is driving home here is that there eventually comes a time when the rubber must meet the road. All the studying in the world is useless if we never take the opportunity to practice it in our lives. Eventually, we must apply what we learn. What good is filling our own cup if we never take the time to pour it into others? Ecclesiastes 3:1 tells us this.

There is a time for everything, and everything on earth has its special season.

I was reminded of this fact just recently. I am an avid reader. Have been since I was a kid. These days, some of my favorite authors include Craig Groeschel and Max Lucado. I enjoy the smooth writing styles of these gentlemen along with the uplifting messages they provide. Each of them is a Christian author and their manuscripts support scripture and help show how to better apply certain aspects to our lives. I was reading one of their latest books and found myself unable to move on from a certain chapter. The chapter dealt with evangelism. First, it described the kind of person who is over-the-top preaching God to others, whether they want to hear about Him or not. You know the kind I'm talking about. In your face, yelling about hellfire and brimstone, screaming at you to repent because we're in end times. Now I know God can use anything for His glory, but I personally am turned off by this approach and feel like it turns more people away from hearing the gospel than brings people to it. I found myself smiling smugly as I read this part of the chapter, looking down my nose at these extremists.

Then the author described another kind of believer. The one who has a great relationship with Christ (*check!*). The one who feels he/she lives a Godly life (*check!*). The one who openly shares their faith when the time is appropriate (*well... two out of three ain't bad*). I found myself convicted by this message. For the believer I claim to be, and for all the Bible studies and supplemental books I read, and for all the Holy podcasts I listen to…if I'm being honest with myself, I rarely share my faith with others. Even when the opportunity presents itself. I've read and studied enough to be able to talk about my relationship with Christ and the joy it's brought me for days on end. But I haven't. And I don't. Why not? Is this something that would take me out of my comfort zone? Am I scared of being rejected? Probably *yes* and *yes*. This really started to weigh on me. I took it to God in prayer and asked for some guidance on this.

Two days later, I was car shopping and found the make and model I was looking for online. I called the local dealership to see if it was still available. I talked to a salesman (we'll call him Sam). He said it was and I said I would see him in ten minutes. I arrived at the dealership and Sam had the fob in hand and said, "Let's go for a drive." We jumped in the vehicle and took off up the interstate. Sam and I made small talk for a while. Then he hit me with a statement I wasn't expecting. He said, "You act like you live a blessed life."

Blessed life? Okay, that's Christian-ese, right? You don't hear that term every day. Was this my crack in the doorway to share my faith? After all, I had been praying for clarity on this. Maybe God was providing the opportunity. Here goes nothing.

"I do live a blessed life, Sam. God's been very good to me." There. It was done. Now the words were hanging out there like when you told someone in middle school you had a crush on them and then waited. And waited. And for me, am still waiting for some of these replies. But it didn't take Sam long to chime in. "God's been good to me, too!"

There it was. I was in! The conversation had begun just that easily. "How so?" I prompted. Sam went on to tell me how things had been rough in life for a while, but he had turned it all over to God and He had helped him turn his life around. He was now living for God's glory and not his own. We both shared stories of God's goodness in our lives. Sam even told me to keep driving and not turn around at the agreed-upon exit to head back. We were like two long-time friends on a road trip, sharing our faith and our struggles with one another.

We finally returned to the dealer lot, and I told him I'd take the vehicle. He said he would draw up the paperwork and be back with me in a few minutes. While Sam was working on that, I prayed. I thanked God for giving me this opportunity to make a new friend and to share my faith. Then I had an overwhelming feeling that this was not enough. I thought to myself, *What more do you want, Lord? I just shared my faith. Is that not enough?* And then I felt God saying to me, *"No. Pray for him."*

Easy enough, I thought. I'll just add this to my list of items I already planned on praying about before I went to bed that night. Then I felt God stirring my heart again. *"No. Pray for him. And pray with him."*

With him? In public? People may see us. Or even worse, make fun of us! And how do I even ask someone I just met if I can pray with them? Is this crossing some kind of line? But I remembered this is what I prayed for. And I truly felt God was answering my prayer. And I wanted to be obedient to Him. The worst that could happen was that Sam would say no to the group prayer. And then tack on some hidden costs to my car loan just to stick it to me.

Sam drew up the paperwork. I signed it and was the proud new owner of a pretty sweet ride. Sam shook my hand and thanked me for the business. I probably shook hands way too long while trying to figure out what to say next. Finally, I just blurted out, "Sam, may I pray for you?" Sam immediately smiled back at me and nodded his head. "Yes, Sir." I had never done this in my life, but I laid my hand on Sam's shoulder, and he returned the gesture. Then we both bowed our heads, right outside the showroom floor and I prayed. I prayed for his walk with the Lord and for him to continue to overcome the obstacles he was facing. I asked God to bless him and his family and to continue using him for His glory.

I haven't seen Sam since. We've emailed a few times, but that's it. I don't know what Sam's takeaway from our interaction was, but I know I feel like a better man after this. God showed me that reading and studying are crucial to growing in this world. There is wisdom in balancing study and action. Putting down the books now and then to apply what we've learned, is why we study at all. What good do any book smarts do us if we never apply them to our lives in order to help others and to glorify Him?

Discussion Questions

1. Are there any areas of your life where you have prepared long enough? Where might God be calling you to act on what you have learned?

2. Think of a skill that you possess. How might you use that talent to glorify God?

3. How do you think this quote by King Solomon fits into the Grand Narrative?

CHAPTER 13

I Never Knew You
A Story of Jesus

Up to this point, I've shared different stories from the Bible that scared me. We've covered everything from talking animals to exorcised demons. This chapter is not about a certain story that scared me, but a specific line that did the trick. It's one short sentence spoken by none other than Jesus. In Matthew 7:23, He says,

> *Then I will tell them clearly, 'Get away from me, you who do evil. I never knew you.*

On the surface, this is an unassuming passage. Sure, Jesus had a right to talk to folks this way. You know the ones I'm referring to, the religious bigots, the scum of the Earth, those that chose to bad-mouth Jesus every chance they got. Of course, Jesus never knew them. They never gave Him the opportunity. The only problem is that these are not the kinds of people Christ is talking about. If we backtrack a few verses to Matthew 7:21-22, here is the earlier part of Jesus' statement.

> *[21] Not all those who say that I am their Lord will enter the kingdom of heaven. The only people who will enter the kingdom of heaven are those who do what my Father in heaven wants. [22] On the last day many people will say to me, 'Lord, Lord, we spoke for you, and through you we forced out demons and did many miracles.'*

These weren't the heathens and blasphemers you may expect to be lumped into the category of folks that Jesus said He never knew. These were the law-abiding, righteous, well-respected community leaders. The kind that were always in the public eye, praising God and performing good deeds. If Christ didn't know these folks, then what chance did any of the rest of us non-miracle-performing Christians have?

And listen to the condescending tone that I feel is implied here. Jesus could simply say, *"I'm sorry…you just don't cut it as far as righteousness goes. I appreciate the effort, though."* No. He says, *"I never knew you."* Talk about harsh! Not only would you have just found out that you wasted your efforts, but now Jesus is claiming to have never even known you? This is definitely not the all-inclusive Jesus that came to offer salvation not just to Jews, but to everyone, is it?

It is. This is the same Jesus who came to save *everyone* who would seek and accept Him. This passage is not about the man speaking. It's about whom He's speaking of. There were folks during His time who were all consumed with keeping the law.

Sadly for them, that didn't leave a lot of time for this Jesus character roaming the countryside, healing the sick, restoring sight to the blind, and raising the dead. Two groups of people who would fit this mold were the Pharisees and Sadducees. Both were religious societies of Judaism during Jesus' time on Earth, with the Pharisees being the more influential of the two. Both groups, along with a few other sects at the time, cared more about reciting scripture, performing certain rituals, and observing ancient customs than they did listening to the radical ideas Jesus was sharing.

Jesus was busy teaching people about concepts that were qualitative, not quantitative, like faith, hope, and love. The Pharisees preferred the quantitative measures so that they could not only see how they measured up when it came to religion, but how they measured up against others around them. And when they did, they not only bragged about their mighty religiousness, but they looked down their noses at others who they deemed not quite on their religious level.

These people, the Pharisees, Sadducees, and the like, experienced religion with their heads. Jesus was inviting folks to experience Him with their hearts. And he was adamant about distinguishing between the two. I think one of the reasons He felt so strongly about this is that He knew it was going to continue today. We still have Pharisees and Sadducees running around, telling everyone how to worship God. Only now we call them legalists. Legalists are the ones who claim to know Jesus by strictly adhering to rules that they believe make them right with God. And they're quick to tell anyone who will listen what they should or shouldn't do to be accepted by Him.

But it's not the rules that make us right with God. It's our personal relationship that does that. Throw all the rules out the window. If you don't know Christ on a personal level, none of the rest of the stuff that goes along with being a Christian matters. Because that's all it is…stuff. It begins and ends with a personal relationship with Jesus. And it's as simple as talking to Him and asking Him to be your Savior. And if you're not in a place in your life where you're ready for that, He welcomes you to simply talk to Him. Ask Him questions. Get to know Him.

The folks Jesus was referring to in the above scripture were mostly performing religious acts so that they could look good in front of their peers. They were using the law as a stepping stone to elevate themselves. It was never about Jesus. That is why He was referring to these folks as doing evil. Not only were they missing the point of what Jesus was teaching, they were teaching the opposite in His name.

The concept is simple, yet still hard to fully comprehend. Christ wants a personal relationship with us. He wants to know us and for us to know Him. This relationship is the single most important aspect of Christianity…knowing and accepting Jesus. Too many times, I hear the phrase, *"You need to accept Christ as your personal Savior."* And I wholeheartedly agree with that. But we forget to offer the advice of getting to know Him first. After all, how can anyone accept something or someone they don't know? Christ realized this. And He simply wants to get to know His children, so that they can, in turn, know His limitless love for them and then *want* to accept Him into their lives. In fact, He desires nothing more than to know us and save and bless us. But our hearts must be right, and that's where growing to know Jesus comes into play. The more we grow in our relationship with Him, the more He prepares our hearts. And the better prepared our hearts are, the more He pours out His blessings.

It's a brilliantly orchestrated causal chain of events that God has planned for us. We will be blessed with Godly success when our hearts are like His. Our hearts are like His when we accept Jesus as our Savior. We accept Jesus as our Savior when we spend time in relationship with Him and come to truly know Him. Do you see the divinity of this pattern? It begins and ends with Jesus, with blessings along the way. It starts with establishing a relationship with Jesus, which leads to Him using you to successfully carry out His plans in your life, which leads to eternal life, which can never be taken away.

Allow me to share a quick story about being in a right relationship with God and allowing Him to change your heart. Back in 2009, I self-published my very first book. It was a children's book titled *Raccoons' Christmas*. I muddled through the writing, editing, publishing, and printing process, which were all foreign to me at the time. When all the work was finished and I was convinced I had made every mistake I could possibly make along the way, the books arrived.

This was a bittersweet moment. I looked at all the boxes of freshly printed books that had been dropped off on my front porch, smiled, and thought to myself, *I did it*! I'm a published author! I'm standing here looking at a thousand copies of *Raccoons' Christmas*. And then reality kicked in. *I have a thousand copies of Raccoons' Christmas!* I know nothing about marketing or sales. I just assumed if I created the book, people would buy them. You know, the whole *Field of Dreams* philosophy. Nothing could have been further from the truth. I decided to not press the panic button just yet and to hit up all my family and friends to buy some books. And that worked to some degree. Now, I only had nine hundred and fifty more books to move.

I remember looking at the mountains of unsold books on my dining room table and wondering if my family would ever forgive me for investing our hard-earned money into this crazy venture. That's when I decided to pray. Sad, right? *That's* when I decided to pray. When I was desperate. When I needed God's help. Not that there's anything wrong with that. I just feel like I should have included God earlier in the planning phase of all this. I vividly remember the prayer. Well, it wasn't as much of a prayer, as it was a business proposition for God. I told God that I had a lot of books. And these were good books because they told the story of salvation on a child's level, so obviously it would be a good thing for kids to read this book. So naturally it would be a good thing if He made sure that every copy sold. That way, His word would get into the hands of children, and I would make money. Embarrassingly, I remember using the phrase with God that this would be a *win-win* for us!

To my disbelief, book sales did not take off. About a week later, I walked past the books again and the piles now felt like they were somehow growing. I decided a follow-up prayer was in order. I confessed to God that deep down I knew my previous prayer was selfish. I asked Him to just forget about that one. I now had a new proposition for Him. I was such a changed man and so unselfish now that I was no longer worried about making money on these books. I prayed that I just sold enough to break even. And I felt proud of this prayer. I was such a selfless Christian. After all, I wasn't looking to get rich anymore. I just didn't want to lose money. Surely, this was a fair prayer.

After another week of Raccoons' Christmas selling like whatever the opposite of hotcakes is, I decided it was time for a final heart-to-heart talk with God. I was feeling pretty broken at this point, realizing I had no business being in this industry. I remember telling God that our money was spent. If we didn't make another dime off the books, it was okay. I knew he'd provide for us in the future like He always had in the past. I also prayed that if God used the message of salvation in this book to reach one kid, or adult for that matter, and help point them to Christ, then it was worth the investment of time, money, and energy. And I meant every word of that.

Looking back, I know God used this process to help change my heart. He wanted my motives to be pure. He wanted me to realize that this endeavor was for His glory and not my own. Immediately following this prayer, it was as if an elephant had taken its enormous foot off my chest. I could breathe again. Priorities were back in line. Literally, one day later, I was contacted by a local TV station, newspaper, and radio for interviews to help promote the book. I vividly remember calling the local newspaper back to accept the offer but to also ask why they wanted to interview me now. You see, I had reached out to them a few weeks before and was shot down. The answer I received as to the change of heart? *"I don't know. I got to work this morning and had a sticky note on my desk to give you a call to set up an interview."* I never found out who wrote the sticky note, and I honestly don't care. I know that God used someone to move this project forward. God also placed other special people in our path to help us as well. These folks hosted book signings, left reviews online, and shared our journey on social media. When it was all said and done, *Raccoons' Christmas* ended up making money and launched a new career for me.

It's no coincidence that our success came after I opened up to God and turned over my problems to Him. It goes back to what we discussed at the beginning of the chapter. It doesn't matter what we do or how we go about doing it. If we do not have a personal relationship with Christ, all we are and all we do is in vain. Whether you are in constant communication with Jesus or it's been a while since you've spent any personal time with Him or even if you've never spent any time with Him, I encourage you to do just that. It can be as simple as telling Him how your day is going. He'd love to hear from you. When it's all said and done, I hope it's not said of any of us that Jesus never knew us.

Discussion Questions

1. Reflect. Have you ever done anything for the sole purpose of being noticed or appreciated? What did you do? Why was this so important to you? How did things turn out?

2. Are there any areas in your life where you feel like you may just be going through the motions in your relationship with Jesus? Do you find yourself more concerned with *following the rules* of Christianity than you are with having a personal relationship with Christ? Explain.

3. How do you think this story of Jesus fits into the Grand Narrative?

CHAPTER 14

Easter Saturday
A Story of One of the Darkest Days in History

Okay, it's time to shake things up a bit. This next chapter is not about a Bible story that scared me or confused me or even one that I used to manipulate for my personal interests. This one is about a period of time that the Bible seems to gloss right over. It's a certain day during Holy Week that never seems to get any attention. We recognize Ash Wednesday as the first day of Lent and as a reminder of our mortality. Then there's Maundy Thursday when we commemorate the Last Supper taking place and remind ourselves of the importance of humility and service to others. Then we have Good Friday, the day Jesus gave His life for ours. Followed by Easter Sunday, the day Jesus defeated death and changed the game forever. Did you notice something missing in this sequence? What about Saturday? What happened then? Why don't we talk about it? How dark of a time must this have been for Christ's followers? There you have it. That's your buildup. Now it's time for my commentary on Easter Saturday.

I love Easter. It, along with Christmas, are my favorite times of year. Both have special meanings and are worthy of celebration. Just a few years back, I had the pleasure of watching my dad channel his inner Phillip as he and twelve others reenacted the Last Supper at a Maundy Thursday Service. I was honored to narrate a Good Friday Service at my own church. And the Sunrise Service my family and I attend every Easter Sunday is typically my favorite worship time of the year. That's a lot of celebrating. Thursday, Friday, Sunday. But again, what about Saturday? This day seems to be lost in translation when we honor this time. After all, what does it have to offer?

Thursday, we remember Jesus and His disciples breaking bread together one last time. Friday, we recall the pain and suffering Christ endured on his way to, and upon, the cross. Sunday, we treasure His resurrection as He walked out of the tomb, stared death in the face, and said, "Is that all you've got?" But again... what about Saturday?

In my opinion, that specific Saturday in world history had to have been the most discouraging of them all. Jesus, the teacher, helper, friend, and Messiah, was gone. Everyone who had put hope in Him suddenly had nothing. He had come into the world, turned it upside down, shared God's radical message, performed miracles beyond what anyone had ever seen, debated with politicians, counseled with wise teachers, and partied with the lowest of sinners. He was loved by some and hated by others, but make no mistake, his presence was felt by all. And now He was gone.

Gone forever? No one was really sure. Even though He foretold what would happen to him, including coming back again, doubt crept in. Matthew 16:21 tells us,

> *From then on Jesus began to speak plainly to his disciples about going to Jerusalem, and what would happen to him there – that he would suffer at the hands of the Jewish leaders, that he would be killed, and that three days later he would be raised to life again.*

Did you catch that? Jesus spoke *plainly.* Not in parables or riddles or industry lingo that was above his disciples' heads. He clearly told them what was about to happen to Him. Not only the unthinkable aspect of his execution but the unimaginable facet of His return. But the disciples were still confused. And their faith wavered. Nobody knew for sure that Jesus' return was imminent. So how dark must that Saturday have been? For the believers, the one to whom they had dedicated their lives, put their faith in, and given all their hope, was no longer with them. Perhaps He never would be again. They just didn't know. Or they did, but still chose to doubt.

I can't imagine a darker time in history than that time between the crucifixion and the resurrection. But when you really stop to think about it, that day is nothing more than a microcosm of the world we live in today. Look at the comparisons. Jesus is not physically with us these days, but He has promised to return. Many of us, because we can't see His face or have a two-way conversation with Him, question His existence.

Because we face tragedy in our lives today, we sometimes choose to focus on our temporary circumstances and not the everlasting life that is part of the package deal of knowing Jesus. Some scoff at the fact that He is actually real. Others know of Him, but since He's out of sight, He's out of mind. And others love Him, and though fear and doubt creep into our minds from time to time (and it happens…we're human), we quickly revert our eyes to the cross, or better yet…the empty tomb, and are reminded that we're just living in a very long Saturday.

Sunday will assuredly come and we will see Him again. As we learn in Revelation 21:4,

He will wipe away all tears from their eyes, and there shall be no more death, nor sorrow, nor crying, nor pain. All of that has gone forever.

So take a moment to celebrate Saturday this Easter. I'm going to use it as a tool to strengthen my faith. Just like He's done once before, He tells us that even though He's not with us right now, we will most certainly see Him again. That's what Easter is all about. He punched death in the mouth so that we would never have to succumb to it. Death has no sting because of what Christ endured on the cross.

There is not one place in the Bible where Jesus turns someone away. And there's not one place in the Bible where Jesus says something and does not follow through on it. Easter is a personal time. What Jesus did, he did for each of us individually. If you're struggling with something in your life right now, I invite you to focus less on the problem and more on our Savior. Saturday doesn't last forever. Sunday is inevitable.

Discussion Questions

1. That Saturday must have been a long one. How is your patience these days? Is there anything you are anxiously waiting on God to bring you to or deliver you from? How are you dealing with the perceived delay? Is your patience building character?

2. We may not always agree with God's timing, but do you believe He knows best? And do you believe that His timing is perfect? Why or why not?

3. How do you think the story of Easter Saturday fits into the Grand Narrative?

CHAPTER 15

Hair Today, Gone Tomorrow
A Story of Absalom

The next Biblical childhood scare I had came not so much from a story itself, but from a specific scene that plays out. Meet Absalom. He's the son of King David. He's a really bad dude with a head full of long, luscious, flowing locks. I'm picturing Fabio with an even *fuller* body of hair. And for anyone reading this who may not be familiar with who Fabio is, google *Harlequin Romance cover model* and you'll get a pretty good visual.

Anyway, this is an evil guy. So evil that he cannot wait to inherit the kingdom from his father and starts a rebellion to take the crown by force. But it's not the short-lived battle between father and son that gave me pause for concern when I was younger. It was how it all ended for Absalom. 2 Samuel 18 sums it up nicely for us.

⁹ Then Absalom happened to meet David's troops. As Absalom was riding his mule, it went under the thick

> *branches of a large oak tree. Absalom's head got caught in the tree, and his mule ran out from under him. So, Absalom was left hanging above the ground. [10] When one of the men saw it happen, he told Joab, "I saw Absalom hanging in an oak tree!" [11] Joab said to him, "You saw him? Why didn't you kill him and let him fall to the ground? I would have given you a belt and four ounces of silver!" [12] The man answered, "I wouldn't touch the king's son even if you gave me twenty-five pounds of silver. We heard the king command you, Abishai, and Ittai, 'Be careful not to hurt young Absalom.' [13] If I had killed him, the king would have found out, and you would not have protected me!" [14] Joab said, "I won't waste time here with you!" Absalom was still alive in the oak tree, so Joab took three spears and stabbed him in the heart. [15] Ten young men who carried Joab's armor also gathered around Absalom and struck him and killed him.*

Are you picturing this like I am? A guy with long flowing hair is riding a donkey through the woods. There's an apparent low-hanging branch that catches him *by his hair*. The donkey keeps going while Absalom is yanked off and left dangling in midair. Maybe subconsciously this is the reason I always sported a Johnny Unitas crew cut when I was younger. Short hair rarely gets you into trouble. Okay, back to Absalom. Here he is, hanging helplessly by his hair, alone in the forest. Then one of David's men sees the opportunity to vanquish their foe. Even though David told his men to go easy on his son, they decide to take matters into their own hands. They decide Absalom deserves

Death by Bon Jovi...Shot Through the Heart! My publisher begged me to not use this joke, but I couldn't help myself. Joab sticks not one, not two, but three spears through the defenseless man's heart. And if we're reading this text correctly, that doesn't kill him! Another ten guys come along and take shots, striking Absalom until he dies. Then they unceremoniously toss him in a pit. The thought of a man, hanging by his hair from a tree, being stabbed multiple times through the heart, and then being beaten to death is not what I immediately think of when I ruminate on the Bible. But this mental image eventually creeps up on me.

So why did this story make it into the pages of the Bible? What can we learn from this? Let's take a look at the character of Absalom, shall we? 2 Samuel 14:25 tells us this.

Absalom was greatly praised for his handsome appearance. No man in Israel was as handsome as he. No blemish was on him from his head to his foot.

I already hate this guy. Not just because he's a bad guy with an axe to grind with his old man. It's because he is so good-looking! I have nothing in common with him. It's hard for me to connect with this character. We're drawn to most characters in the Bible because they are just as flawed as we are. We resonate with their failures and mistakes. We appreciate the fact that we're not the only ones who seem to mess up on a continuous basis, yet are still used by God.

Absalom is unbelievably handsome. And he knows it. So, what does he do with these looks? Become a successful male model and give the proceeds to charity? Sell glamour shots of himself with inspirational quotes written on them to inspire others? Start a health care program to help others improve their images? No. He uses his looks for personal gain. 2 Samuel 15 illustrates just how slimy Absalom was. People were drawn to Absalom by his physical appearance, and he would use these opportunities to manipulate them.

> *[1] After this, Absalom got a chariot and horses for himself and fifty men to run before him. [2] Absalom would get up early and stand near the city gate.[a] Anyone who had a problem for the king to settle would come here. When someone came, Absalom would call out and say, "What city are you from?" The person would answer, "I'm from one of the tribes of Israel." [3] Then Absalom would say, "Look, your claims are right, but the king has no one to listen to you." [4] Absalom would also say, "I wish someone would make me judge in this land! Then people with problems could come to me, and I could help them get justice." [5] People would come near Absalom to bow to him. When they did, Absalom would reach out his hand and take hold of them and kiss them. [6] Absalom did that to all the Israelites who came to King David for decisions. In this way, Absalom stole the hearts of all Israel.*

Please tell me you caught the whole *Gosh, Shucks* routine. *"I wish someone would make me judge in this land. Then I could solve all your problems for you."* Yes, that second line was implied, but it's most certainly what Absalom meant. After hearing that, folks probably thought he wasn't just handsome. He was humble and selfless as well. Who wouldn't want to support someone like that? The only problem was, he wasn't genuine. He possessed only one of the three aforementioned qualities. The question that we should ask of this story, and even more so from the image of Absalom hanging by his hair with three spears protruding from his chest is this:

What do we do with what God has given us?

God blessed Absalom with beauty. This guy, had he been born during our time, would be the hands-down winner of People Magazine's Sexiest Man Alive contest year in and year out. And what did he do with his attractiveness? He used it to manipulate, control, and negatively influence those around him. And he did a good job. His revolt led King David into hiding for a while. But it didn't last. That's what happens with ill-gotten gains. They're only temporary. He could have done so much with what God blessed him with. And he was next in line to be king if only his patience had matched his looks. We see this sort of thing happen time and time again throughout history. Men and women use their gifts, their skills, and talents, to take control. Or to wield some sort of power over others. And history also teaches us that these times and these people don't last long. Absalom will be remembered as someone who tried to take what wasn't his. And almost succeeded. But in the end, he ultimately failed. And one of the most handsome men to ever walk the planet died in what some consider the most embarrassing and dishonorable death imaginable. And if we're being honest, so often when we abuse the gifts we've been given, they come back to hurt us in the end.

Maybe not to the extent that Absalom experienced, but they can sting nonetheless. There have been millionaires who hoarded their money, only to say on their deathbed, the money made them miserable. Riches, athletic prowess, business acumen, beauty, sense of humor, diligence, wisdom...whatever the gift may be, when we start treating it like something to solely give us an advantage over others as opposed to helping others, it can become an albatross around our necks. Either we use our gifts for good or our gifts will start to control us and ultimately lead to our demise. So, let's revisit that question once more before we close out this chapter.

What do we do with what God has given us?

What are your spiritual gifts? What are you good at? What do you enjoy? Where do those last two activities intersect? What gives your life meaning? What do you feel you have to offer the world? I could continue peppering you with these kinds of questions, but you get the point. Simply put, what did God bless you with that he wants you to offer the world? Romans 12:6-8 tells us this.

> *⁶ We all have different gifts, each of which came because of the grace God gave us. The person who has the gift of prophecy should use that gift in agreement with the faith. ⁷ Anyone who has the gift of serving should serve. Anyone who has the gift of teaching should teach. ⁸ Whoever has the gift of encouraging others should encourage. Whoever has the gift of giving to*

others should give freely. Anyone who has the gift of being a leader should try hard when he leads. Whoever has the gift of showing mercy to others should do so with joy.

If you're good at teaching, are you imparting your wisdom to others? If you're good at motivating others, are you empowering them? If you're good at making money, are you donating to charity or tithing? Are you using your gifts to invest in God's kingdom here on earth? Or are you using your gifts for personal gain? Take some time to think about this. It can be convicting. Please don't mishear me. We all need to make money and support ourselves and our families and we want to live comfortable lives. But where does our motivation for what we're doing come from? Does it come from a need to impress others? A need to be the most popular person in the room? A need to have the nicest house or car on the block? A need to be the most educated person in the class? Or does it come from a longing to serve God? A desire to give back a small portion of the gift He's bestowed upon us? One of my favorite quotes from Eleanor Powell, and one that I think sums up this discussion nicely, is this:

"What we are is God's gift to us, what we become is our gift to God".

James 1:17 reminds us that,

Every good action and every perfect gift is from God.

When it's all said and done, we can't take anything with us when we leave this world. We can store up treasures in Heaven, but we can't take anything with us. This is just one more reminder that we are stewards of what God has blessed us with. We're not the owners. Everything we have is on loan to us. God gave us our talents and skills for a reason. To glorify Him. And when our time on earth is done, I really want to be able to hear Him say to each and every one of us, *Well done, good and faithful servant.*

Discussion Questions

1. What are you doing with the gifts God has blessed you with? Are you blessing Him back?

2. Do you check your motives in all situations? What drives you to do what you do? Selfish ambition or Godly determination?

3. How do you think the story of Absalom fits into the Grand Narrative?

CHAPTER 16

The Original Walking Dead
A Story of the Resurrection

I watched *Night of the Living Dead* when I was a kid and had nightmares for weeks. It was an old movie even at that time but was still ultra-creepy. *It's just a movie*, I kept reassuring myself. *These things don't happen in real life. Man up!* This kind of self-talk eventually helped lead me back to unencumbered sleep. Then I stumbled across an obscure Bible passage in Matthew. Chapter 27:52 to be precise.

> *⁵² The graves opened, and many of God's people who had died were raised from the dead. ⁵³ They came out of the graves after Jesus was raised from the dead and went into the holy city, where they appeared to many people.*

If you read this and are picturing a scene from AMC's *The Walking Dead*, then you're not alone. This is literally describing dead people walking into Jerusalem and being seen by many. To put this into context, this happens after Jesus gives up His life on the cross. There was an earthquake, the curtain in the temple was torn in two (which is one of my favorite metaphors in the Bible, symbolizing that there is nothing separating us from Christ and His love for us), the graves opened, and the dead rose and made their way to the Holy City.

For anyone thinking that I may be exaggerating the horror of this scene, please see the very next verse.

> [54] *When the army officer and the soldiers guarding Jesus saw this earthquake and everything else that happened, they were very frightened and said, "He really was the Son of God!"*

There you have it. The soldiers who were just mocking and ridiculing Christ on the cross were then frightened for their lives. I'm sure there was nothing in the Roman Soldier handbook that prepared them for what to do in case of a zombie uprising. And here's an interesting fact that makes the story even more frightening. Many theologians believe that this whole scene played out over the course of a few days. It is believed that as soon as Jesus drew His final breath, the veil tore in half, the earthquake occurred, and graves were opened. But the buried didn't rise just yet. Jesus was the first to be resurrected from the dead. Acts 26:23 tells us,

> *that the Christ would die, and as the first to rise from the dead, he would bring light to all people.*

And in addition to that, I Corinthians 15:20 shares,

> *But Christ has truly been raised from the dead—the first one and proof that those who sleep in death will also be raised.*

If we are to believe in scripture, then here is clear evidence that Christ had to rise first before any others were resurrected. So, the earthquake busted open the graves, most of them thought to be in stone, and the bodies lied there for another few days until Jesus left the tomb. Then they got up and paraded into Jerusalem. Again, where many eyewitnesses reported what they saw.

Now, even though you didn't ask for it, you have a clearer timeline of the course of events that took place. So, what do we make of all this? Why did the others rise from the grave after Jesus? What is our horrific takeaway? Personally, I think God was demonstrating what is today a popular communication axiom. *Say it clearly. Say it consistently. And say it creatively.* Do this and you have an excellent chance of successfully delivering your message to your audience. God's message? John 3:16.

> *God loved the world so much that he gave his one and only Son so that whoever believes in him may not be lost, but have eternal life.*

Was the message delivered clearly? Read John 14:6.

> *Jesus answered, "I am the way, and the truth, and the life. The only way to the Father is through me."*

It doesn't get too much simpler than that. Jesus didn't mince words. He kept it short and sweet. He left no room for interpretation or tweaking the message. *"I AM THE WAY."*

Was the message delivered consistently? Jesus covered many topics in His teaching during His ministry, but He talked more about the Kingdom of Heaven than anything else. It was woven into almost all His lessons, parables, and speeches. His audiences changed and His venues altered. But His message remained consistent. Eternal life awaits those who put their faith in Jesus. Often, He refers to His Father's Kingdom as *"at hand"* or *"near"*. He even refers to it as *"come upon you"* in Matthew 12:28. His main message, more often than not, centered around the last part of John 3:16. *Eternal life*. It is what He wants for all of us.

Was the message delivered creatively? How does one argue that it was not? Christ dies on the cross. The veil in the Temple miraculously tears on its own, symbolizing nothing will ever stand between us and God. A freak earthquake occurs, opening nearby graves. Three days later, Jesus walks out of the tomb, defeating death once and for all. This changes everything. Sin and death are beaten. Everything Jesus had taught was being fulfilled. And to add the cherry on top of this sundae, just as one more reminder of what Christ's resurrection means to the rest of us...other bodies rise from the grave. The resurrection train has left the gate! *All aboard!* Jesus had to go first. Now all of us can take the ride. And when I now think about these folks rising from their graves and marching toward Jerusalem, I picture less of Michael Jackson's *Thriller* video and more of a celebration of the transformed. A pilgrimage for all of us. Leaving a quick layover in death, and making our way, first class, to our final destination. Our eternal home with our Father who can't wait to welcome us face-to-face.

Discussion Questions

1. The preceding story can be very polarizing. Some may view it as frightening while others may view it as a beautiful promise fulfilled. Do you tend to see the positive or the negative in life's situations? Give an example.

2. Do you believe that Christ leads the way in your life? Are there any areas where you may be getting ahead of Him? If so, what can you do to pivot?

3. How do you think the story of the open graves fits into the Grand Narrative?

CHAPTER 17

Why Doesn't God's Script Match Mine?
A Story of John the Baptist

Another Bible story that scared me was the tale of John the Baptist. More specifically, the tale of the end of John the Baptist. As a kid, John was one of my favorite characters. Truth be told, he probably still is today. To me, John always appeared to be larger than life and on fire for the Lord. And he was cousins with Jesus, which is pretty cool, too. John and Jesus knew each other since childhood and John even baptized Jesus. Then John decided to call out King Herod for wanting to divorce his wife and marry Herodias, his sister-in-law and niece. John called this unlawful and was very outspoken about the king's transgressions. As if this relationship couldn't get any more convoluted, Herodias then prompts her daughter to seduce Herod so he will give her anything she asks for. The plan is executed to perfection and Herodias' daughter then asks Herod for…John the Baptist's head.

When I read the story the first time as a child, I thought to myself, first of all…gross. And then second of all, there's no way John the Baptist goes out like this. Herod won't touch him. After all, he's Jesus' cousin. They're family. They're blood. They share the baptism bond. Jesus definitely has his back. Then I continued to read. John the Baptist is arrested. Then beheaded. The good guy dies. The bad guys live happily ever after (for all we know). And Jesus? He's nowhere to be found. This story scared me, but in a different way. There was nothing supernatural or creepy about this story. But it was still scary to me. Scary because I felt like John was a great person. He stood up to the evil that he saw happening. And he was killed for his troubles. And Jesus could have stopped this. After all, He's Jesus. But He didn't. It felt dismissive. Neglectful. Apathetic. Three words I thought I'd never use to describe Christ.

Maybe I needed to continue reading the story. Yes, John was killed. No, there were no repercussions for Herod or Herodias. But maybe Jesus wasn't done yet. After all, He'd raised Lazarus from the dead. He could surely perform this miracle again. Especially for His own cousin. Yes, Jesus was going to save John and then smite this incestuous couple! So I kept reading. And here's what happens in Matthew 13:14 when news of John's death reaches Jesus.

When Jesus heard what had happened to John, he left in a boat and went to a lonely place by himself.

Huh? That's it? Where's the outrage? Where's the vengeance? Where's the miraculous resurrection? How can He let this stand? Instead of plotting revenge or planning to revive His cousin, Jesus grieves. He never calls on His angels to smite Herod. He never breathes life back into John. He grieves. He simply mourns the loss of His friend. *Why?* Why grieve when He could have done something about it? After years of struggling to find an answer to this question, I finally figured it out. The reason Jesus didn't save John and punish Herod?

It's the same reason, due to a heart murmur, I had to say goodbye to my four-legged best friend, Bailey, last year.

It's the same reason my daughter, Kayla, was born three months premature, weighing a whopping two pounds, twelve ounces, at birth.

It's the same reason wars rage, children go to bed hungry at night, and civility seems to die a little more each day.

The reason? *God doesn't follow my script.*

And after some reflection on that statement…I could not be more grateful for that fact.

Here's why. As one of my favorite pastors stated one time, *"If we knew what God knows, we would do what God does."* Am I glad that Bailey isn't by my feet when I write every day? No. Am I glad Kayla had to be confined in an incubator for her first month of life while tubes jammed down her throat and nose kept her alive? Did I enjoy her mother and I not even being able to hold her? Absolutely not. Do I enjoy war, hunger, or disrespect? Of course not. And I will never completely understand why they exist. But that's just the tip of the iceberg of things I don't understand. We see only a glimpse of the vast expanse of God's infinite wisdom. And I don't agree with everything He does. And I let Him know that. But I know He's in control. I know He loves us. And I know he uses all circumstances for good. I'm not trying to trivialize any heartbreak or sorrow that anyone is going through. I've had my share as well. But I trust that one day I'll understand why we had to be hurt or broken or embarrassed or suffer the way we did. Romans 11:33 reminds us,

No one can explain the things God decides or understand His ways.

While we cannot understand why God doesn't follow our playbook or comprehend why He allows bad things to happen to good people, He sometimes gives us a small glimpse of His plans. It broke my heart to bid farewell to Bailey. But this opened the door for a new pet. We welcomed Maple into our home sometime later. She is a black and tan Cavalier King Charles Spaniel and was not only the runt of her litter, but she was also the only one that had not been adopted out of all her siblings. No one wanted her until we came along. I'm glad we could make her part of our family. And Kayla's premature entry into the world? Once we received word of my wife's torn placenta and the gravity of the situation, I initiated my first prayer chain. And I included every single person I knew. This meant involving friends of mine who are atheists and agnostics. I told them what had happened and what I wanted from them as a personal favor. And they obliged. And I know these folks well enough to know they weren't lying to me when they said they prayed. I can look back on this event now that Kayla is all grown up and a specimen of fine health and smile at the fact that God may have used this situation to have a conversation with the folks who didn't even believe in Him.

And how about John? Why didn't Jesus spare him from the grave, like He did for his good buddy, Lazarus? Alas, I don't have a definitive answer for this one. But I have my theories. Maybe it was a timing thing. I often reflect on the King James version of John's famous quote about Jesus from John 3:30.

He must increase, but I must decrease.

Perhaps John was at peace with this seemingly early exit. Again, I just don't know. But maybe he understood that he had played his part and had rolled out the carpet for One who is greater than he. This may have been the *decreasing* to which he was referring. And his reward for his role? Eternal life in Heaven. There's your storybook ending! And let's not forget about Lazarus. Yes, Jesus resurrected him. But the part of the story that is not shared with us and that I never gave much thought to is this. Lazarus eventually died. We all do. And when we know our Savior, we know where we're going.

As for war and famine, and incivility. As for the parents who have to bury a child. As for the homeless, the addicted, the abused. I don't know why these occur. But I do know the One who does. And one day I'll get to talk to Him face-to-face and get the answers to these burning questions. And I trust that they, as improbable as it sounds now, will make sense then.

Until then, I will continue to remind myself that I know very little. My scope is narrow. My judgement is often flawed. I take comfort in this…

"If we knew what God knows, we would do what God does."

Discussion Questions

1. Think back to a time when God's plans for you were vastly different than yours. How did things turn out?

2. Is it difficult to submit your ways to God's ways? How do you react when your prayers aren't answered in the manner you expect them to be?

3. How do you think the story of John the Baptist's death fits into the Grand Narrative?

CHAPTER 18

Angels Among Us
A Story of Elisha

The following story is one of my favorites. Is it a Bible story that made me scared? Yes. So, it fits within the parameters of this book. But it's a tale that didn't make me scared for myself. Or even for the good guys in this chapter. This story made me scared for the bad guys. Allow me to explain by first sharing some scripture with you. 2 Kings 6:8-18 sets the table for us:

> [8] *Now the king of Syria was at war with Israel. After conferring with his officers, he said, "I will set up my camp in such and such a place."* [9] *The man of God sent word to the king of Israel: "Beware of passing that place, because the Arameans are going down there."* [10] *So the king of Israel checked on the place indicated by the man of God. Time and again Elisha warned the king, so that he was on his guard in such places.* [11] *This enraged the king of Syria. He summoned his officers and demanded*

of them, "Tell me! Which of us is on the side of the king of Israel?" ¹² *"None of us, my lord the king," said one of his officers, "but Elisha, the prophet who is in Israel, tells the king of Israel the very words you speak in your bedroom."* ¹³ *"Go, find out where he is," the king ordered, "so I can send men and capture him." The report came back: "He is in Dothan."* ¹⁴ *Then he sent horses and chariots and a strong force there. They went by night and surrounded the city.* ¹⁵ *When the servant of the man of God got up and went out early the next morning, an army with horses and chariots had surrounded the city. "Oh no, my lord! What shall we do?" the servant asked.* ¹⁶ *"Don't be afraid," the prophet answered. "Those who are with us are more than those who are with them."* ¹⁷ *And Elisha prayed, "Open his eyes, Lord, so that he may see." Then the Lord opened the servant's eyes, and he looked and saw the hills full of horses and chariots of fire all around Elisha.* ¹⁸ *As the enemy came down toward him, Elisha prayed to the Lord, "Strike this army with blindness." So he struck them with blindness, as Elisha had asked.*

To paraphrase, the king of Syria was upset because his plans to conquer Israel kept being thwarted. When he found out it was Elisha who was the cause of all this, he located his foe and sent his army to take him out. His army arrived and surrounded the city in which Elisha was currently residing. Elisha's servant then took his early morning stroll, sipped his freshly brewed coffee, and suddenly realized they're not alone. He saw the vast Syrian army and all their weapons surrounding them. He ran back to warn Elisha and most likely started figuring out an escape plan. But Elisha didn't bat an eye at their present circumstance. Instead, he turned to his assistant and delivered one of the greatest tough-guy lines in Biblical history. And I can't help but read this line in John Wayne's voice every time. He said, *"Don't be afraid. Those who are with us are more than those who are with them."*

Such a cool line for any action movie aficionado. But this didn't seem to comfort his servant. And I can't say that I blame him. Yes, it's a reassuring phrase. But at this point, to him, they're just words. And it's Elisha's words versus the Syrian army! *Ahhh, but is it?* Elisha then prayed that his assistant's eyes may be opened to see what's really happening around them. And just like that, the servant looked up and saw *hills full of horses and chariots of fire all around Elisha.* Suddenly, the Syrian army is outflanked, outnumbered, and outmatched. God's spiritual army, also referred to as the Heavenly Host, was there ready to do battle. And they had been there all along. It's just that the servant, and everyone else besides Elisha, could not see them.

Elisha wasn't worried that the Syrians had them surrounded. Because through his faith, he could see that they weren't the only ones surrounding the city. God's angel army was there, too. And according to Hebrews 11:1, that's what faith is:

Faith means being sure of the things we hope for and knowing that something is real even if we do not see it.

It's up for debate as to whether or not Elisha could actually see the angelic infantry or that because of his great faith, he just knew they were there. But what he did know was that his servant needed some encouragement. He prayed that his buddy would be able to see what he knew was there, and God obliged. I'm sure this put the servant's mind at ease, but here's where the story gets even more interesting. These Holy troops never lifted a finger against the Syrian army. Elisha prayed again and the Syrian army went blind. Elisha then tricked them into believing that this was not the city they were looking for. Kind of like the old Jedi mind trick, but it was a lot easier because none of them could see. He told them to follow him, and he would take them to Dothan, but instead tricked them and led them into Samaria, right into the hands of the king of Israel. From there, Elisha took mercy on his enemies and encouraged his king to not only spare the lives of their prisoners but to throw a feast for them and then send them on their way. They did this and these soldiers never returned to face them again.

The question now begs, if Elisha could just offer up a prayer and have the Syrians' eyesight taken from them, what was the spiritual army doing there? I have two theories to offer. The first is that the Heavenly Host was there purely for Elisha's servant to witness. It appears he may have needed a nudge in the faith direction and what better way to help someone believe than to give them a quick glimpse behind the divine curtain? But would God go to all this trouble and situate all these angels, enough to cover the hills, for just one person's sake? Absolutely. This is the same God who gave His own Son for each one of us individually. Nothing is too elaborate for our God when it comes to Him showing His love for us.

The second theory I have is that this is commonplace in the spiritual realm. Perhaps we have these angel armies surrounding us in every situation we find ourselves in. Monday through Sunday. Twenty-four hours a day. Psalm 34:7 tells us,

> *The angel of the Lord camps around those who fear God, and he saves them.*

This is the theory I most readily subscribe to. Is it because I binge-watched *Highway to Heaven* back in the 1980s? Yes. Is it because I translate Psalm 34:7 literally? Also, yes. I believe there is a spiritual realm we cannot readily see. And I believe in evil spirits and demons. But I don't worry about them. Because I also believe that the same angel armies that protected Elisha still work to protect you and me today. Based on a lot of my poor life decisions, I'm sure my guardian angels collect some sort of overtime pay or extra vacation days, but nonetheless, I believe they are here. And they guide and protect us. And if you're like me and feel like you may need an extra angel or two to watch over you, rest easy. The New King James translation of Hebrews 12:22 comforts us with his jewel,

> *But you have come to Mount Zion and to the city of the living God, the heavenly Jerusalem, to an innumerable company of angels,*

Innumerable? As in *too many to count!* Just like God's love for us and His mercy toward us, the supply is limitless! And this ties back in nicely to Elisha's earlier statement, *"Those who are with us are more than those who are with them."* With God on our side, we are never in the minority. Remember that the next time you're feeling depressed, defeated, scared, or unloved. You are not alone. In fact, you have an angelic army by your side. They are guiding you, protecting you, and most of all, rooting for you!

Discussion Questions

1. Do you believe there are angels among us? Why or why not?

2. How much of a difference do you believe having faith makes in your life?

3. How do you think this story of Elisha fits into the Grand Narrative?

CHAPTER 19

God > Behemoth + Leviathan
A Story of Job

Let's now discuss a frightening Bible story about bad things happening to a good person. Let's talk about Job. Even if you're not too familiar with the Bible, there's a good chance you've heard of Job. He's so popular even in modern culture, there's a phrase based on his life. *"He or she must have the patience of Job."* Job was a Godly man, and seemingly because of this wonderful attribute, ended up suffering greatly. All stemming from a supernatural discussion between God and the devil. Job 1:8-12 shares this,

> *⁸ Then the Lord said to Satan, "Have you noticed my servant Job? No one else on earth is like him. He is an honest and innocent man, honoring God and staying away from evil." ⁹ But Satan answered the Lord, "Job honors God for a good reason. ¹⁰ You have put a wall around him, his family, and everything he owns. You have blessed the things he has done. His flocks and herds are so large*

> they almost cover the land. *¹¹ But reach out your hand and destroy everything he has, and he will curse you to your face." ¹² The Lord said to Satan, "All right, then. Everything Job has is in your power, but you must not touch Job himself." Then Satan left the Lord's presence.*

When I read this as a child, I couldn't shake the feeling that the devil antagonizes God and God takes the bait. I know that sounds crazy. And it even sounded crazy to me at the time, but it still felt that way. Why would God begin to entertain the thought of discussing one of his children's well-being with Satan? And according to the story, God brings up Job first. It's as if He were bragging about him. Did the devil see an opportunity to wreak havoc and decide to run with it?

In the next few verses, Job tragically proceeds to lose his property, all his children, and his health. And God allows this. His best friends, Eliphaz, Bildad, and Zophar, try to convince him that he has obviously done something wrong to incur God's wrath like this and that he should repent. His wife takes a different approach. She tells Job to curse God and die. Not the greatest support group to have during a time of suffering.

The age-old question surfaces during this chapter. Why does God allow bad things to happen to good people? Was he being careless or callous with Job's welfare? Was a deal with the devil more important than caring for His child? For too long, I became so hung up with these questions that I overlooked the part of this story where God actually talks to Job.

God speaks to Job from a whirlwind. Many theologians believe that the whirlwind represents God's fury and anger.

While not refuting that belief, I interpret God speaking from the whirlwind a bit differently. I believe God was speaking from the whirlwind symbolically. I imagine this is one of His ways of showing that He is ever-present, even in the eye of whatever storm we're facing in life. He is not a distant God. He is ever-present, no matter how bad a situation seems.

During this talk, God references two scary creatures, Behemoth and Leviathan. Depending on which translation you read, both these beasts can come across as very cryptic and very frightening. But what are they? Various Bible scholars and pastors disagree on exactly what they represent. Some believe that the Behemoth represented a hippopotamus. And that Leviathan represented a crocodile. Others believe that Behemoth and Leviathan were dinosaurs. Still others believe them both to be mythological creatures. Regardless of what they really are, God paints a frightening picture of them. In Job 40: 15-18, God says this about Behemoth,

> *[15] Look at Behemoth, which I made just as I made you. It eats grass like an ox. [16] Look at the strength it has in its body; the muscles of its stomach are powerful. [17] Its tail is like a cedar tree; the muscles of its thighs are woven together. [18] Its bones are like tubes of bronze; its legs are like bars of iron.*

And this is what He says about Leviathan in Job 41:7-9,

> *[7] Can you stick darts all over its skin or fill its head with fishing spears? [8] If you put one hand on it, you will never*

forget the battle, and you will never do it again! ⁹ There is no hope of defeating it; just seeing it overwhelms people.

Both these monsters are being described to show that man has no hope of conquering either beast. But now look at what else God says about them. Job 40:19 refers to the Behemoth, claiming this,

It is one of the first of God's works, but its Maker can destroy it.

And in Job 41:10, this is what God has to say about Leviathan,

No one is brave enough to make it angry, so who would be able to stand up against me?

Here are two creatures that are described as completely overpowering to man. Untouchable, untamable, and unstoppable. Yet God assures us He could easily destroy both. At the same time. With both hands tied behind His back. He's using this analogy to remind Job *and us* that however overwhelming our circumstances become, however frightening or intrusive our enemies are, they are no match for our God. Nothing is. Nothing ever has been. Nothing ever will be.

Listen to some of the questions God poses to Job in Job 40:8-14.

⁸ Would you say that I am unfair? Would you blame me to make yourself look right? ⁹ Are you as strong as God?

Can your voice thunder like his? ¹⁰ If so, then decorate yourself with glory and beauty; dress in honor and greatness as if they were clothing. ¹¹ Let your great anger punish; look at the proud and bring them down. ¹² Look at the proud and make them humble. Crush the wicked wherever they are. ¹³ Bury them all in the dirt together; cover their faces in the grave. ¹⁴ If you can do that, then I myself will praise you, because you are strong enough to save yourself.

Once upon a time I read these questions and pictured an angry and vengeful God, giving Job an earful because he dared to question God's intentions. Now, I read this, seeing a loving and reassuring God, letting Job *and us* know that he/we can't handle everything that comes his/our way in life. But God can. Nothing is too hard for the Lord. Nothing is too difficult. Nothing is too daunting. Nothing comes as a surprise. He is completely and totally in control. It may not always feel that way to us, but the entire book of Job is a complete reassurance of this truth.

What once felt like a story about a God that didn't care about his people, is now, in my opinion, one of the most uplifting books in the Bible. It shows not only God's love for us, but also his unrivaled power to guide, direct, and protect us from any giant we may face in life. Whatever Behemoth, Leviathan, disease, despair, dilemma, or tragedy we face, we will never face it alone. God is with us and God is for us. He vehemently states that over and over again in this story.

Need more proof? Revisit the first two chapters of Job. When God is talking to Satan in Chapter 1, He tells the devil he can do what he wants, but he is not allowed to touch Job. Then in Chapter 2, the devil renegotiates and is given permission to make Job suffer with physical ailment, but once again, God provides parameters. The devil is not allowed to kill Job. I bring this up because I think this dynamic is fascinating and comforting at the same time. This is God and the devil talking. Ultimate good versus ultimate evil. God sets the ground rules, and the devil obeys them. He doesn't try to be sneaky or manipulative and slip something past God. Because he knows he can't. He obeys God because he knows God's power. And as much as he may despise it, he recognizes God's authority.

Yes, bad things are going to happen to us. That's life. But instead of blaming God or praying for a pain-free life, try dwelling on an excerpt from my favorite verse from Job 2:10,

Should we take only good things from God and not trouble?

God is not a genie in a magic bottle that we just go to when we want something. He's not here to grant our every wish. He is so much more than that. He does not promise us a pain-free life now, but it's coming. And until then, He reminds us that He's with us in every step of the most painful journeys of our lives. He's in control of our circumstances. What we can't understand, He can. And He'll explain it all to us one day. Until then, He continues to reassure us that He's got our backs more than we will ever know. And He asks us now and then to *"have the patience of Job."*

Discussion Questions

1. What are the *Behemoths* and *Leviathans* in your life right now? Do you believe God is bigger than your fears?

2. Are you able to praise God during your struggles? If so, how? If not, what changes may be needed to do so?

3. How do you think the story of Job fits into the Grand Narrative?

CHAPTER 20

Saul's Scary Situation
A Story of King Saul

The next story we're about to break down was scary to me as a kid and is still scary to me today as a semi-well-adjusted adult. Anytime someone delves into witchcraft or sorcery to try and summon the dead, it's creepy. I know that almost all the other chapters in this book have dealt with stories that were once scary, but when broken down, are a bit tamer. This one remains unsettling. So why are we discussing it? Because while the story may still be disturbing, these days, I have a new perspective on what to take away from this ominous tale. But before we dive into that, allow me to provide some backstory. King Saul is worried, (some even describe him as paranoid) about his upcoming battle with the Philistines. Saul has turned away from God and God is not answering his prayers like he used to. Samuel, who served as a priest, prophet, and judge, (he was a triple threat) and used to work with King Saul, has since died and is no longer able to pass on information from God to Saul.

Saul, in his delusional wisdom, decides to consult a medium to speak to Samuel from beyond the grave to gain the insight that God has decided not to share with him. Basically, the guy is looking for a workaround, eliminating God from the equation. It's important to point out that mediums and sorcerers, the exact type of people he was looking for, had been banished and their practices were recently outlawed...*by Saul!* But by his logic, I guess desperate times called for desperate measures. And Saul had to know what was in store for him in the looming battle! Here is exactly how it plays out in 1 Samuel 28:4-20:

⁴ The Philistines came together and made camp at Shunem. Saul gathered all the Israelites and made camp at Gilboa. ⁵ When he saw the Philistine army, he was afraid, and his heart pounded with fear. ⁶ He prayed to the Lord, but the Lord did not answer him through dreams, Urim, or prophets. ⁷ Then Saul said to his servants, "Find me a woman who is a medium so I may go and ask her what will happen." His servants answered, "There is a medium in Endor." ⁸ Then Saul put on other clothes to disguise himself, and at night he and two of his men went to see the woman. Saul said to her, "Talk to a spirit for me. Bring up the person I name." ⁹ But the woman said to him, "Surely you know what Saul has done. He has forced the mediums and fortune-tellers from the land. You are trying to trap me and get me killed." ¹⁰ Saul made a promise to the woman in the name of the Lord. He said, "As surely as the Lord lives, you won't be punished for this." ¹¹ The woman asked, "Whom do you want me to bring up?" He answered, "Bring up Samuel." ¹² When the woman saw Samuel, she screamed. She said, "Why have you tricked me? You are Saul!"¹³ The king said to the woman, "Don't be afraid! What do you see?" The woman said, "I see a spirit coming up out of the ground." ¹⁴ Saul asked, "What does he look like?" The woman answered, "An old man wearing a coat is coming up." Then Saul knew it was Samuel, and he bowed facedown on the ground. ¹⁵ Samuel asked Saul, "Why have you disturbed me by bringing me up?" Saul said, "I am greatly troubled. The Philistines are fighting against me, and God has left me. He won't answer me anymore, either by prophets or in dreams. That's why I called for you. Tell me what to do." ¹⁶ Samuel said, "The Lord has left you and has become your enemy. So why do you call on me? ¹⁷ He has done what he said he would do—the things he said through me. He has torn the kingdom out of your hands and given it to one of your neighbors, David. ¹⁸ You did not obey the Lord; you did not show the Amalekites how angry he was with them. That's why he has done this to you today. ¹⁹ The Lord will hand over both Israel and you to the Philistines. Tomorrow you and your sons will be with me. The Lord will hand over the army of Israel to the Philistines." ²⁰ Saul quickly fell flat on the ground and was afraid of what Samuel had said. He was also very weak because he had eaten nothing all that day and night.

A scary scene, right? Like something straight out of *The Conjuring*. And when you start to study this passage and break it down, guess what? It gets even more frightening. First off, many theologians and Biblical scholars believe that the spirit that was summoned and came to them *out of the ground*, was in fact, *not Samuel*, but a demon posing as Samuel. So right there, this just became a lot more disturbing. Time and again, scripture illustrates that the spirits of God come down to us from Heaven. These same illustrations show that spirits that come from the earth are from Satan and are demons. Another reason many believe that this was not the real Samuel, is that if it were, and he did come back and speak to Saul and prophesy for him, then it would mean that Saul found a loophole to exclude God and get what he wanted without Him. It just doesn't work that way with an omniscient God.

The next fun fact is that many Bible historians believe this medium to be a fraud. You know, just like Whoopi Goldberg's character in *Ghost*. Why? Because as soon as she sees the spirit claiming to be Samuel, she screams. As if she's not accustomed to seeing the dead rise. If this was her full-time job and she was legitimate, this kind of scene should be mundane to her. But she freaks out. Saul, who can't even see the spirit at this point, tells her to calm down. That's how startled she is.

And if this story doesn't keep moving the creepy meter forward, the spirit's message to Saul is the icing on the cake. Saul wants to know what the future holds. What time should they schedule their victory party after defeating the Philistines? The answer he gets from this spirit is haunting. There will be no victory celebration. Within twenty-four hours, the king and his sons will all be joining the spirit in death. Kind of reminds me of when the ominous grim reaper-looking ghost of Christmas Future shows Ebenezer Scrooge the fate that awaits him. Only, Saul's fate was sealed while Scrooge was able to rectify his future.

This story has all the usual suspects to make up a creepy story. You have the paranoid king who misplaces his trust, the witch (although the Bible never actually refers to her as one) who turns out to be a fraud, and the demon who was summoned and wreaks havoc. Again, not a story that we covered in Sunday School as a kid. So why is it in the Bible? What lessons can we glean from this *Tale from the Crypt*? Like so many others, I believe this is a cautionary tale. The medium and King Saul are two characters that we do not want to emulate.

What did the medium do wrong? She lied. She pretended to be something she was not. And she found herself in a position in which she did not want to be. First, she was frightened by the spirit she didn't expect to see. And then she was frightened when she realized Saul's true identity. Both could have cost her her life. God calls us to be authentic and genuine. Timothy 3:13 warns us,

But people who are evil and cheat others will go from bad to worse. They will fool others, but they will also be fooling themselves.

I would argue that this describes the medium's situation in this story. Psalms 101:7 tells us,

No one who is dishonest will live in my house; no liars will stay around me.

Lying or pretending to be something we are not dishonors God. He calls on us to be men and women of integrity. Proverbs 12:22 reminds us,

The Lord hates those who tell lies but is pleased with those who keep their promises.

And lastly, in Proverbs 12:19 we learn,

Truth will continue forever, but lies are only for a moment.

Lies and misrepresentation will always catch up with us. Just like they did with the medium. Deceiving others ultimately dishonors God and discredits us.

And what about King Saul? What can we learn from him? Simply put, we learn to trust in God and God alone. To coin a poker phrase, we must be *all in* with God. Saul disliked not hearing from God on a regular basis, so instead of self-reflection, examining what may have caused this alienation, and trying to make it right with God, Saul chose to move on to plan B. He decided to take his trust, his hope, and his anxieties. All his dreams and insecurities. His future planning. His thoughts and his fears. Everything he had. He chose to invest it all in something other than God. Instead of surrendering them to God, he moved on. He put his trust in a fortune-teller. And the rest, unfortunately for King Saul, is history.

It's easy to look down our noses and cast condescending thoughts toward the fallen king, but many of us are a lot more like Saul than we'd like to admit. How often do we pray for something, wait, hear nothing, and then go try to obtain it ourselves? I'm not saying we shouldn't pray *and* work toward our goals. After all, James 2:17 tells us,

In the same way, faith by itself – that does nothing – is dead.

God calls for us to work. He calls on us to be the hands and feet of Christ in this world. But Proverbs 3:6 cautions us to,

Remember the Lord in all you do, and He will give you success.

The difference being, we must keep Christ first and foremost in our hearts and on our minds. Everything we do should be for His glory and honor.

And let's be honest. Sometimes it feels like God is close to us and sometimes it feels like He's a million miles away. The next time you feel this way, please remember two things. Nothing can separate you from God's love. He's never far away from us. And secondly, maybe God is giving you an opportunity. Perhaps it's a chance to grow your faith or to seek Him more diligently. One of my favorite quotes of all time is this, *"When you are going through difficulty and wonder where God is, remember that the teacher is always quiet during the test."* King Saul tried to remove God from his agenda and paid the price. Deuteronomy 4:29 shares,

> *But even there you can look for the Lord your God, and you will find Him if you look for Him with your whole being.*

With your whole being. Again, we need to be *all in* with God. He does not want, and will not accept, anything less. He addresses those who are not fully committed in Revelation 3:15-16 when He says,

> *[15] I know what you do, that you are not hot or cold. I wish that you were hot or cold! [16] But because you are lukewarm – neither hot, nor cold – I am ready to spit you out of my mouth.*

Have you ever wondered what would make the God of the universe puke? The answer is being lukewarm. God takes very seriously our commitment and loyalty to Him. He is totally invested in us and yearns for it to be a two-way street. He gave us free will. The choice is ours. Will we desire Him completely, even when it may seem entirely contrary to worldly wisdom? Will we seek Him wholly when others argue why we shouldn't? Will we exclusively follow Him when other paths appear to be quicker and easier? Will we take matters into our own hands and try to cheat the system, like Saul did?

God invested all He had in you. He gave all He has to you. He only wants you to follow His lead and trust in Him. It won't always be easy. It won't always make sense. But He assures us it is the only path to righteousness. And it will be worth it in the end.

Discussion Questions

1. Have you ever taken shortcuts in your life when you felt like God was taking too long to answer your prayers? How did that work out?

2. Have you ever lied to get what you wanted? Was the outcome worth it?

3. How do you think this story of Saul fits into the Grand Narrative?

CHAPTER 21

A Curious Case of Context
A Story of Jesus

This next story is about a Biblical character who I originally felt acted very un-Christlike. Why would this be an issue? There are a lot of characters in the Bible who act like this. My pause for concern here is that the character in this story is Jesus, himself. He has a conversation with a Canaanite woman, and I felt during my first few readings, that He comes off a bit rude. It takes place in Matthew 15:21-28.

> *[21] Jesus left that place and went to the area of Tyre and Sidon. [22] A Canaanite woman from that area came to Jesus and cried out, "Lord, Son of David, have mercy on me! My daughter has a demon, and she is suffering very much." [23] But Jesus did not answer the woman. So his followers came to Jesus and begged him, "Tell the woman to go away. She is following us and shouting." [24] Jesus answered, "God sent me only to the lost sheep, the people of Israel." [25] Then the woman came to Jesus*

again and bowed before him and said, "Lord, help me!" ²⁶ *Jesus answered, "It is not right to take the children's bread and give it to the dogs."* ²⁷ *The woman said, "Yes, Lord, but even the dogs eat the crumbs that fall from their masters' table."* ²⁸ *Then Jesus answered, "Woman, you have great faith! I will do what you asked." And at that moment the woman's daughter was healed.*

So let me get this straight. A woman comes to Jesus and asks for healing for her daughter. And Jesus responds. First, by ignoring her. Then, by dismissing her. And finally, by basically calling her a dog. This seems completely out of character for the Son of Man. Yes, He eventually gives her what she asks for, but wow, did she have to earn it! This story did not sit well with me for years. Then I learned about this fantastic concept called *context*.

Context is described as *the circumstances that form the setting for an event, statement, or idea, and in terms of which it can be fully understood and assessed.* In other words, context helps paint a truer picture of what's really happening in any given scenario. Do me a favor. Skim back and reread the previous passage. Feel free to start at verse 24 and visualize this back-and-forth dialogue between Jesus and the woman. Go ahead. I'll wait.

Now, I'm going to ask you to reread this passage one last time. And I want you to visualize the scene again. Only this time, imagine it with both Jesus and the woman…*smiling.*

Did this change your perception of the event? Instead of what once felt like Jesus talking down to someone, it now comes across as banter. Jesus shows the woman and quite possibly his onlooking followers, the true extent of this woman's faith. Jesus knows her heart better than she does. And sometimes vocalizing our faith can make it stronger, not only for us but for those watching what we do and say. This isn't an isolated incident, either. Jesus often challenged others with questions like this, to help prove or solidify their intentions.

And let's not forget how the story ends. Jesus heals the daughter of this woman. This is a wonderful moment of foreshadowing. Jesus reminds the woman that His priority is the people of Israel. Taking His eyes off the prize, so to speak, would seem like abandoning His mission. Hence the line, *"take the children's bread and give it to the dogs"*. He was referring to the Israelites as the children and anyone else (including the woman) as the dogs. But in a very revealing moment, Jesus heals the non-Jewish woman's daughter. Why? Because that's who Jesus is. He does not just love us. He *is* love. The Biblical definition of love is, *a selfless, sacrificial, and unconditional commitment to the well-being of others, reflecting the divine nature of God's love as revealed in Scripture.* Jesus tells us in John 15:12,

This is my command: Love each other as I have loved you.

And this scene with the woman is just one more example that He gives us regarding this. Think about this the next time it may be hard for you to love your neighbor (which He also calls for us to do). You know, the neighbor who thinks differently than you. The one who acts differently than you. The one who doesn't fit into your plans at the moment. The one who may not love you back. The one that you consider unworthy. The one like the woman with whom Jesus had a conversation.

Despite His followers literally begging Him to tell the woman to go away, Jesus took the opposite approach. He gave this woman His most valuable commodity. He gave her His time. Time is more precious than money or anything else you may deem valuable. Money and material possessions can be earned and lost. Once time is gone, it's gone forever. To magnify this situation, Jesus knew His days on earth were numbered and that every second of His mission was crucial. He chose to stay and have a conversation with a non-Jewish woman. He showed her love. He used her as an example of true faith to those watching. And He heard and answered her plea for help.

Remember this the next time you feel like God is testing you. Or questioning your motives. Sometimes He intentionally makes us uncomfortable to help expose us to a side of ourselves we didn't know existed. God will stretch us at times to help us see our potential. He will also use us to be an example to others. He will meet our needs. And He will always make time for us.

When I now read this passage, I don't see Jesus being rude or dismissive at all. I see Him as I always see Him. Loving others. Caring for others. Unselfishly giving His time to those who didn't make an appointment or bother getting on His calendar ahead of time. Helping others develop and strengthen their faith. Teaching those around Him. And forever changing the lives of the non-Jewish woman and her daughter. Mark 10:45 says this,

In the same way, the Son of Man did not come to be served. He came to serve others and to give his life as a ransom for many people.

Yes, ultimately Jesus gave His life to save ours. But before his trip to the cross, He gave His life to enhance ours. He did this through His day-to-day interactions with people. He was constantly teaching, serving, and helping others. He valued that non-Jewish woman that day as much as He values you and me. He loved that non-Jewish woman as much as He loves you and me. And He would love nothing else than to spend time with you and me just like He did with that non-Jewish woman. Even when His followers and friends told Him to move on, He didn't. Even when we give Him reasons to not love us, He won't stop. We mean that much to Him. I hope you make some time today to spend with the Lord. Just like in the previous story, our God has an open-door policy. He will never arrive late and make you wait. He will never reschedule a meeting with you. And He will never, under any circumstance, refer to you as a dog and mean it.

Discussion Questions

1. Do you believe Jesus loves you and has your best interests at heart even when He feels distant? Even when you fail?

2. Scripture consistently reminds us that Jesus loves you. But do you believe he *likes* you? There's a difference. Why or why not? (Spoiler: He loves you *and* likes you. But we often overlook the latter.)

3. How do you think this story of Jesus fits into the Grand Narrative?

CHAPTER 22

You'll Never Go in The Water Again
A Story of Jonah

Jaws is one of the greatest movies ever made. It was the first film to earn over one hundred million dollars at the box office and is considered the first summer blockbuster ever. It won Oscars for Best Film Editing, Best Original Score, and Best Sound. Additionally, it was nominated for Best Picture and is considered to be the film that made Steven Spielberg a household name. And after all these years, it still resides on the American Film Institute's Top 100 Movies List. Why is this movie so popular? Why did fans literally line up in the streets to get a seat in the theater to watch this? Because it paints a realistic portrayal of fear. A creature from the ocean terrorizes folks. That means the fear is compounded. Yes, most of us are scared of this giant shark with a taste for blood. But most of us are also, to a certain degree, scared of the ocean. The sea is not our home. It is not our most comfortable environment. We're land lovers.

Or *landlubbers*, as an 18th-century pirate would call us. We can breathe on land. Our feet can touch the ground on land. We can usually see what's around us on land. And we typically don't have to worry about being attacked by a giant monster at any given time.

Jaws invoked both a conscious and unconscious fear of an unfamiliar and uncomfortable environment, as well as a bloodthirsty killer with no remorse. No one was safe if you ventured into the water. In fact, one of the tag lines for the original movie was, "You'll never go in the water again." So, it's no wonder that the story of Jonah and the Whale (one that we actually *did* cover in Sunday School) was so scary to me as a kid. To be honest, it still creeps me out today. This story shares the same elements as *Jaws*. The ocean and all its uncertainty and a giant sea beast. But I now understand that the real story of Jonah doesn't start until Act 2, once he's taken up residence in the belly of the beast.

The Book of Jonah begins with God telling Jonah to go to the city of Nineveh. The people there are doing some really bad things and God is not happy with them. But this is the God of second chances, so instead of immediately punishing this group, he decides to send Jonah there to warn them to turn away from their evil ways and to turn to God. Jonah decides he doesn't want to participate in this plan. Instead of talking to God about this or pleading his case as to why someone else may be better suited for the job, Jonah doesn't say a word. He goes to the docks, buys a ticket to ride, and heads out to sea. But instead of sailing to Nineveh like God had commanded, he sets sail to Tarshish, a whopping 2500 miles away! That's right. Jonah's plan was to run away from God. A God who knows all and sees all. God gives Jonah some time and then intervenes. He sends a massive storm and everyone on board the boat fears for their lives. When they realize it's Jonah's fault and that God is doing this to them because of him, they start to examine their options. Jonah sees the writing on the wall and tells them that since it is truly his fault, they should throw him overboard to save themselves. To the sailors' credit, they don't take him up on his offer at first, but when other plans fail, they reluctantly toss him overboard. Then two things happen. The storm subsides. And Jonah is swallowed by a whale.

I don't know what would be scarier. Being tossed into the middle of the ocean to drown. Treading water until your arms are too weak and you give up on living. Seeing a monstrous whale heading toward you and knowing your fate was sealed. Being eaten by the enormous sea creature. Or surviving for three days in the dark, wet insides of the beast. In my opinion, each one of these moments is just as horrific as the next. But, also in my opinion, this is where the real story begins.

Jonah, who had previously run away from the Lord, finds himself somehow still alive inside the whale. So, he decides to do what he should have done before. He prays. Jonah 2:7 shares,

When my life had almost gone, I remembered the Lord. I prayed to you, and you heard my prayers in your Holy Temple.

And God listens. And God answers. Jonah 2:10 shows His response.

Then the Lord spoke to the fish, and the fish threw up Jonah and on to the dry land.

This is a beautiful illustration of man's stubbornness and God's patience. Who knows what would have happened had Jonah not prayed. But the bottom line is that God gave him the opportunity to do so. Just like He was giving the residents of Nineveh.

At this point in the story, it feels like everything is cool between Jonah and God again. Jonah messed up. Jonah rectified the situation. It's time to let bygones be bygones and move forward. But just like all the rest of us, it's only a matter of time before Jonah once again shows the ugly side of his humanity. Jonah heads to Nineveh and starts delivering the message God had given him. Jonah 3:4 shares,

After Jonah entered the city and walked for one day, he preached to the people, saying, "After forty days, Nineveh will be destroyed."

Forty days! The countdown to annihilation has begun. The clock is now ticking. Jonah has done his job and is sure he has pleased the Lord. The King of Nineveh catches word of Jonah's message and believes him. He orders everyone to fast and put on rough cloth to show that they are repentant for what they've done. They are truly sorry and are asking God to forgive them and to change His mind about this whole obliteration thing. For the second time in this story, God not only gives the opportunity for repentance, but He rewards it. He decides to spare the city of

Nineveh and everyone in it. This is great news. Another happy ending. It would have been nice if the Book of Jonah had ended on this note. But it doesn't.

Everyone is happy and rejoicing and celebrating. Except for one man. Yep. You guessed it. Jonah. Instead of celebrating God's kindness to this city…the exact same kindness He had just shown Jonah, he becomes angry. Only this time, instead of running away from God, he confronts Him and says this in Jonah 4:2-3,

> *² He prayed to the Lord, "When I was still in my own country, this is what I said would happen, and that is why I quickly ran away to Tarshish. I knew that you are a God who is kind and shows mercy. You don't become angry quickly, and you have great love. I knew you would choose not to cause harm. ³ So now I ask you, Lord, please kill me. It is better for me to die than to live."*

I would argue that this monologue alone makes Jonah the biggest drama queen in the entire Bible. He is upset because he feels his reputation is now somewhat tarnished. He told them they had forty days to live. Now, that's not true. And he feels upset about this. Like God owes him some sort of apology. And how about the hyperbole in Jonah's last line? *Please kill me?* I'm unsure if this guy's ego is that fragile, or if he is being super dramatic to try to make a point. Either way, Jonah appears to be more concerned with how man views him than he is with how God views him. That's another cautionary tale for us. How often do we seek people's approval over God's. I'd like to say *never*, but the worldly need to be popular and accepted and to be part of the in-crowd sometimes begins to cast shadows on seeking to please God first.

I then love how God responds to Jonah, in a classic counseling move from any Psychology 101 book. He answers his question with a question in Jonah 4:4.

Then the Lord said, "Do you think it is right for you to be angry?"

Fair question. And Jonah never answers Him. Instead, he goes to the east of the city and builds a shelter to wait and see what happens to Nineveh. Listen to what God does next for the man who just blasted him and wished himself dead. Jonah 4:6 states,

The Lord made a plant grow quickly up over Jonah, which gave him shade and helped him to be more comfortable. Jonah was very pleased to have the plant.

Here is another classic example of God's nature. Jonah runs away from God, then yells at God and tells him that he'd be better off dead than to keep listening to Him. And what does God do in return? He does what He can to make Jonah more comfortable. He gives him shade for rest. Jonah was pleased to have the plant. It looks like everything is cool (no pun intended) between God and Jonah again. And this would be a good place to end the story. But wait…there's more. The next day, a worm attacks the plant that God had given to Jonah for shade. The plant dies, it gets uncomfortably hot, and Jonah has a short memory. And he brings his rant before God yet *again*, this time wishing for death *again*. Not just once, but twice!

God then puts back on his counseling hat and asks Jonah another introspective question in Jonah 4:9.

But God said to Jonah, "Do you think it is right for you to be angry about the plant?" Jonah answered, "It is right for me to be angry! I am so angry I could die!"

At least this time, Jonah answered the Lord, although he had nothing to back up his argument. Then the Lord answers. His final words are, in my humble opinion, some of the most impactful ones in the entire Bible. Jonah 4:10-11 says,

[10] And the Lord said, "You are so concerned for that plant even though you did nothing to make it grow. It appeared one day, and the next day it died. [12] Then shouldn't I show concern for the great city of Nineveh, which has more than one hundred twenty thousand people who do not know right from wrong, and many animals, too?"

Powerful stuff. God had sent the plant and then taken it away, all to illustrate the point He was about to make to Jonah. And it's a point that is just as relevant to every single one of us today. We are passionate about worthy causes. We love the people in our lives. We fight for justice. We hate evil. We try to take care of widows and orphans. God sees this and smiles. He's glad we do these things. He's wired us this way and He delights in seeing us live these types of lives. But He also wants us to remember something else. He is more passionate. He loves more deeply. He fights for justice on levels we can't comprehend. He hates evil more than we do. And he comforts His people more than we are capable of. And He doesn't do this to show off or to belittle our efforts. He does this to remind us that we only see a sliver of life during our time in this world. He was in the beginning. He knew us before we were born. And He knows how it all ends. He sees all and knows all, and this allows Him to show the concern and passion that's needed for His causes and His children.

In the end, this isn't a story about a guy who gets swallowed by a whale. Sure, that's an important scene. And a scary scene, hence making its way into this book. But this is a story of a man who was quick to run away from God, quick to become angry with God, and quick to believe his ideas made more sense than God's rationale. It makes me dislike Jonah. Until I realize he and I are a lot alike. I may not physically run away from God, but my guilty conscience will sometimes prohibit me from spending time with Him. I don't yell at God every time I disagree with Him, but I am quick to question His motives when tragedy occurs. Or when my friends or family are suffering. Or I don't get a good parking spot. Or someone ate the last donut. And I do find myself rationalizing with God more than I should. Using the old *if-then* equation. You know the one I'm talking about. *Dear God, IF you let this book become a best seller, THEN I can tithe a lot more*. As I mentioned in an earlier chapter, I find myself using the phrase *This is a win-win situation* with God much more than I should.

God has never used a whale to get my attention or to put me in time-out to allow me time to come back to Him, but I do believe everything that happens is part of His perfect plan. Sometimes I don't move forward because He needs to teach me something. Maybe I need to recheck my motives. Maybe my faith needs strengthening. Maybe I need to learn it's okay to not be popular. Maybe I need to learn how to lose more gracefully. What is it for you? Is there an area of your life you feel stuck in right now? Where is your *belly of the whale*? And what do you think God may be waiting for you to learn?

At the end of the day, we're all a bit more like Jonah than we'd like to admit. But that's okay. Because God assures us that He loves us, will be patient with us, and will always show more concern for us and our well-being than we can ever imagine. Just ask Jonah. Or any of the residents of Nineveh.

Discussion Questions

1. Are there any areas of your life where you feel like you're running away from God? Are there any areas where you may be ignoring Him or shutting Him out?

2. Do you believe that God loves and cares for us and our loved ones even more than we do? Why or why not?

3. How do you think the story of Jonah fits into the Grand Narrative?

CHAPTER 23

The Revelation of Revelation
A Story of End Times and New Beginnings

You know we couldn't finish this book without mentioning what most believers and non-believers alike consider the most frightening Book of the Bible, Revelation. Why does this book scare so many folks? Why do so many people skip this part of the Bible when they're leafing through? It's a glimpse of what the future holds. It tells of a time when all believers will take their rightful place in paradise and good triumphs over evil once and for all. It's a true happily ever after, fairytale ending. So, again, why does it scare us? Because like any good story, there's never an easy or pleasant path to get to the ultimate reward. Heartache, tragedy, adversity, and misfortune always seem to pave the way to a happy ending. Revelation is a prime example of this. And in our short-sightedness, many of us lose focus on the ending and set up camp and dwell in the hardship. I think this is the bad rap that the Book of Revelation has received. It's a story of hope and redemption but is often categorized as a tale of death and destruction. Most of us hate the phrase, *It's going to get worse before it gets better*, because it reminds us that we're going to have to deal with a situation we'd rather avoid. But we need to remember to keep our eyes on the prize. God tells us how the story ends. And if you're a believer, it's the reason to pop the champagne. If you're not, then I can understand why the story can be uncomfortable to read. But God has put this prophecy on paper for a reason. To give non-believers a chance to accept Christ and avoid the dark days ahead. The party awaiting us in Heaven is an open-invitation one. All are welcome.

So, what specifically is disturbing in Revelation? Take your pick. There are a lot of alarming scenes from which to choose. I'll share a few of mine with you. The first example comes from some imagery of the past before we even get to the future. Revelation 12:1-5 paints this vivid picture,

> *¹ And then a great wonder appeared in heaven: A woman was clothed with the sun, and the moon was under her feet, and a crown of twelve stars was on her head. ² She was pregnant and cried out with pain, because she was about to give birth. ³ Then another wonder appeared in heaven: There was a giant red dragon with seven heads and seven crowns on each head. He also had ten horns. ⁴ His tail swept a third of the stars out of the sky and threw them down to the earth. He stood in front of the woman who was ready to give birth so he could eat her baby as soon as it was born. ⁵ Then the woman gave birth to a son who will rule all the nations with an iron rod. And her child was taken up to God and to his throne.*

John, the author of Revelation, is being shown this vision to illustrate what happened in the past to set the stage for what is going to happen in the future. The child being born is Jesus and the dragon trying to eat the child is the devil. Here we have ultimate good versus ultimate evil, but this imagery makes it even more unsettling. Satan wants nothing more than to stop Jesus from His mission. And a seven-headed dragon, lingering around ready to pounce on a newborn baby is as scary of a scene as I can imagine. Not an image we think about during Christmas when we celebrate the birth of our Savior. The vision continues to show the dragon pursuing the woman who gave birth, but she eludes him. Because of this, we receive this warning in Revelation 12:17,

Then the dragon was very angry at the woman, and he went off to make war against all her other children—those who obey God's commands and who have the message Jesus taught.

This is referring to any believers who follow God's word today. Satan couldn't touch Jesus, so he's coming after us as his consolation prize. If he can't destroy God's Son, he will go after all the rest of God's children. All of us who are believers and heirs with Christ. It's easy to chew on this part of Revelation for too long. It's good that we understand that there's a bounty on our heads when we follow Christ. We need to discern and be shrewd and understand that there is evil in this world. But we must remember to keep reading to the end. God wins. Satan loses. End of story. Yes, we need to be vigilant until this day comes. But we know this day is coming. And so does the devil. Revelation 12:12 tells us,

He is filled with anger, because he knows he does not have much time.

I love this line. It's a reminder that God is content because he knows how the story ends. Satan is angry because he knows how the story ends. We need to look to the Book of Revelation as our North Star in life. We need to live in the here and now, but in times of difficulty, we must remember how the story ends.

To ramp up the satanic imagery even more, the next chapter introduces two scary beasts, ushered in by the dragon. One from the sea and one from land. As a kid, the descriptions of these two beasts alone were enough to give me nightmares. As an adult, what they represent is even scarier. Many Biblical scholars and prophecy experts believe the beast from the ocean represents a gentile leader who will rule over a ten-nation coalition. He will possess power given to him by Satan. This is also who many believe will be the Antichrist. The second beast comes out of the earth, which many of these same scholars believe means this leader will be from Israel and have power and cause many to worship the Antichrist. This person is often referred to as the False Prophet.

Scary stuff, but I love what happens in the following chapter. Three angels appear. This reminds me of a quote from Fred Rogers. If you're not old enough to remember Mr. Rogers, google *Mr. Rogers' Neighborhood*. It was a wonderful children's television show where Mr. Rogers taught lessons in caring, kindness and love. His quote was this, "When I was a boy and I would see scary things in the news, my mother would say to me, 'Look for the helpers. You will always find people who are helping.'"

That's exactly what's happening in Chapter 14. God sends helpers to remind us of some rock-solid facts during some tumultuous times. Read what each angel has to say in Revelation 14:7-12.

> *⁷ He preached in a loud voice, "Fear God and give Him praise, because the time has come for God to judge all people. So worship God who made the heavens, and the earth, and the sea, and the springs of water. ⁸ Then the second angel followed the first angel and said, "Ruined, ruined is the great city of Babylon! She made all the nations drink the wine of the anger of her adultery."*
> *⁹ Then a third angel followed the first two angels, saying in a loud voice: "If anyone worships the beast and his idol and gets the beast's mark on the forehead or on the hand, ¹⁰ that one also will drink the wine of God's anger, which is prepared with all its strength in the cup of his anger. And that person will be put in pain with burning sulfur before the holy angels and the Lamb. ¹¹ And the smoke from their burning pain will rise forever and ever. There will be no rest, day or night, for those who worship the beast and his idol or who get the mark of his name." ¹² This means God's holy people must be patient. They must obey God's commands and keep their faith in Jesus.*

Translation from Angel #1: God wins.

Translation from Angel #2: Satan loses.

Translation from Angel #3: Pick a side.

These angels bring us good news, more good news, and then remind us that we have free will to choose who to follow. *We* have free will but have no doubts that the outcome is gloriously predetermined.

Revelation goes on to describe the Great Tribulation, a horrible time of war, famine, persecution, and pain. All this must happen before Christ's second coming. Another scary period for the world. But once again, please keep reading. After the Tribulation is the second coming of Christ. When everything is finished. The final battle is fought and won. Evil dies and righteousness reigns forever. Speaking of evil dying, there is another frightening image in Revelation. But not for us. For Satan and his team. I'm referring to the Lake of Fire. Horrifying to think of a literal lake of fire. It's also affectionately referred to as the Second Death. But we shouldn't be the ones to fear the Lake of Fire. No, Revelation 20:14 tells us it's reserved specifically for Hell and death. While most believe the Lake of Fire is metaphorical, like much of the imagery in this chapter, it serves as another reminder that God has the power to end Hell and death once and for all. Death, Hell, and Satan's days are numbered. Ours are eternal.

Any story worth telling has a sequel. Every ending is a new beginning. Revelation gives us a glimpse behind the curtain to see how the greatest story of all time unfolds. But it's not really the end. Not for anyone who follows Christ. Revelation tells us of a New Heaven and a New Earth. God's Kingdom is constantly expanding. And we will live with Him forever in paradise. Revelation reminds us that times are tough. Times will get tougher. The devil wants nothing more than to keep us from Christ. The devil is angry and desperate and knows he's running out of time. Revelation also reminds us that just like the Western movies I used to watch as a kid, the good guys win. We will triumph over evil and ride off into the sunset to live another day. And another. And another. For eternity.

Hans Christian Anderson famously said, "Every man's life is a fairy tale written by God's fingers." I believe this to be true. Yes, God allows us to suffer. Yes, God allows us to feel pain. Jesus suffered. Jesus felt pain. He wants us to be like Jesus. And just as He brought Jesus home to sit at His right-hand side, He plans on bringing each one of us home as well. It's been His plan from the beginning. Most everyone loves family reunions. And God is planning the greatest family reunion of all time. When all of us, all His children, the complete body of the Church, dwell together forever. Revelation assures us of this.

Discussion Questions

1. Do the stories in Revelation frighten you? If so, what specific concerns do you have?

2. Are you able to move past the prophesied stories of trial and tribulation in the future to appreciate the beautiful ending and new beginning that is promised?

3. How do you think these stories within the Book of Revelation fit into the Grand Narrative?

CHAPTER 24

Surprise Party
A Story of Heaven

For the final chapter of this book, I'd like to leave you on a high note. So I'm going to share a story with you that illustrates how I picture our first day in Heaven will look. I feel like I caught a glimpse of this years ago. My wife, Angie, asked me if I would take her out to dinner one Friday evening. She said she was in the mood for Mexican food. For a guy who can eat his weight in tacos, my answer was an emphatic *Yes!* We drove to the restaurant, parked, and walked inside. As soon as we entered, I was greeted with a thundering "SURPRISE!" from the huge crowd congregated in the dining room. Angie had successfully pulled off a surprise party for my birthday. I was completely caught off-guard. I took a moment to compose myself and then scanned the cast of characters facing me, starting from left to right.

My in-laws were smiling back at me. Next to them, my work colleagues raised a glass to my arrival. Beside them, my college buddies I hadn't seen in years. Down the line, my friends and neighbors from our community. Then my church family. My good friends I've been close with since high school were there. My Fantasy Football league was in attendance, even though our season didn't start for another few months. Bookending this line of loved ones was the rest of my family. Everyone was excited for me. They had all gathered to greet *me*. To welcome *me*. This was my moment. And my favorite people in the world were there to share it with me. And in addition to my friends and family, the party was catered specifically for me as well. Angie had a buffet set up with all my favorite foods. She had a DJ show up to play 80s music and conduct a round of 80s Pro Wrestling trivia later in the night (My friend Mark still brags that he beat me by one question that night).

The night was a blur. I remember hugging and talking and laughing with everyone there. For a short time that evening, everything was right in the world. I was surrounded by my loved ones, and we celebrated together. This is exactly how I picture my first moment in Heaven will be. With the addition of my Cavalier King Charles Spaniel, Bailey, being the first one to run up and jump into my arms and greet me, tail wagging. Then I imagine Jesus will be next to hug me and welcome me home. It may seem egotistical to picture Jesus at your Welcome Party on your first day in Heaven, but that thought could not be further from the truth. Jesus is the one who's throwing this party. He's been planning it since before you were born. And He will be the happiest one to see you on that day. He will refer to you as *good and faithful servant*, throw a party hat on you, toss the confetti, and then introduce you to all the saints and prior sinners.

This party will be the greatest moment of our lives up to this point. And just the beginning of wonderful experiences to follow. Revelation 21:4 promises us:

He will wipe away every tear from their eyes, and there will be no more death, sadness, crying or pain, because all the old ways are gone.

I know some theologians may want to debate with me the intricacies of my party expectations and that's fine. No one knows exactly what Heaven will be like. But I believe I'll see my loved ones and my pets. I believe I'll still be able to enjoy hot-dogs and donuts (without putting on weight). And even if those things are not to be (although I don't know why God would give us things we love in this life and not have them available to us in the next…but I digress), Heaven will still be a perfect place because we will be with our Father for eternity.

That's why it is so important we don't keep our faith to ourselves in this life. The good news of Jesus Christ is to be shared with everyone we know. God didn't make it complicated. He knew we would do a good job of complicating it on our own. Accepting Jesus as our savior equals eternal life. It's that simple. We are saved by our personal relationship with Christ. There's no adding to it or modifying it. Jesus is the answer.

If you have a friend who doesn't know Jesus, plant the seed today. If you have a friend that you want to spend eternity with but hasn't made that commitment to Christ yet, strike up a conversation. Remember, it's not up to you to convert someone. God will handle that. What we can do is help lead others to Him. Be prepared to talk about Him. Answer questions about Him. Live a life that reflects Him. Use the gifts He's blessed us with for His glory. Be ambassadors for Heaven. There is nothing more important to us in this life than making the decision to accept Christ as our Savior. If you haven't done this or if you simply have questions about this, please call me. I'd love to talk with you about this. My email is jay@jaywforeman.com and my phone number is 540-327-6501. My publisher frowned upon providing my contact information, but I overruled him (in a loving way). I want to see you at my Homecoming Party in Heaven. And I want to be in the receiving line at yours.

Discussion Questions

1. None of us know exactly what Heaven will look like. How do you picture it?

2. Are you excited about the gift of everlasting life? Or are you somewhat apprehensive of the unknown aspects of a new life? Why or why not?

3. How do you think Heaven fits into the Grand Narrative?

Final Thoughts

I hope you've enjoyed this book. And I hope one of your takeaways is that the Bible isn't full of scary stories. It's full of hope. And love. And awesome miracles. God's Word is not frightening. At least not to believers. It's comforting. It's reassuring. It's personally directed toward each one of us. There are multiple times when Jesus tells us not to be afraid. Mark 5:36 shares,

> *But Jesus paid no attention to what they said. He told the synagogue leader, "Don't be afraid. Just believe."*

2 Timothy 1:7 reminds us,

> *God did not give us a spirit that makes us afraid but a spirit of power and love and self-control.*

But God also knows our limitations. And He knows that sometimes we will grow anxious or scared. For these times He shares with us Psalm 56:3.

When I am afraid, I will trust You.

What fears are you facing today? Whatever they may be, God doesn't want you to be consumed by them. He doesn't want you to face them alone. He wants you to bring them to Him. 1 Peter 5:7 reassures us.

Give all your worries to Him, because He cares about you.

God doesn't promise to remove whatever is scaring us. He promises to be with us during these times. When we take Him up on this promise, we see that He is so much greater than whatever our problems may be. John 16:33 tells us that He has defeated the world once.

And He's returning one day for an encore. But in the meantime, don't for one second think He's left you or me to fend for ourselves. He is always with us. Just read Matthew 28:20.

Teach them to obey everything that I have taught you, and I will be with you always, even until the end of this age.

I'd like to leave you with a quote about fear. It's not from the Bible. But it fits well as we come to a close. Here are some wise words from everyone's favorite Jedi master, Yoda.

"Fear is the path to the Dark Side. Fear leads to anger, anger leads to hate, hate leads to suffering."

I love this quote. It's powerful stuff. But do you notice what's missing from this equation? God. Yoda describes a slippery slope beginning with fear and ending with suffering. But insert God into this situation at any point and the entire system is disrupted. God can alleviate our fears. God can cool our anger. God can eliminate our hate. And God can remove our suffering. When all is said and done, remember this. Fear is a feeling, not a fact. Fear is fleeting. God is eternal. Fear is a barrier. God is an enabler. Fear is a prison we build for ourselves, and God wants to smuggle in a cake with a key baked into it to help us escape. Finally, fear is a choice. And so is following God. Choose wisely. Choose faith over fear.

Printed in the USA
CPSIA information can be obtained
at www.ICGtesting.com
LVHW021254141124
796130LV00001B/1